ASIAN POLICY

A Twentieth Century Fund Paper

ASIAN POLICY

THE NEW SOVIET CHALLENGE IN THE PACIFIC

BY ROBERT A. MANNING

PP Priority Press Publications/New York/1988

The Twentieth Century Fund is a research foundation undertaking timely analyses of economic, political, and social issues. Not-for-profit and non-partisan, the Fund was founded in 1919 and endowed by Edward A. Filene.

Newm

DS

518

.7

.M34

1988

c-1

Library of Congress Cataloging-in-Publication Data
Manning, Robert A.
  Asian Policy

  "A Twentieth Century Fund paper."
  Includes index.
  1. East Asia—Foreign relations—Soviet Union.
2. Soviet Union—Foreign relations—East Asia.
3. Soviet Union—Foreign relations—1975- .
4. East Asia—Foreign relations—United States.
5. United States—Foreign relations—East Asia.
6. United States—Foreign relations—1981- .
I. Title.
DS518.7.M34   1988   327.4705   88-31634
ISBN 0-87078-245-2
ISBN 0-87078-244-4 (pbk.)

Foreword

East Asia's emergence as the most dynamic economic region in the world has mesmerized the public. Scholars have written extensively on the implications of "the Pacific Century," pointing out that forty years after World War II, which reduced Asia to penury, the region presents the United States with a series of complex challenges generated by its new and vigorous economic strength. Those challenges have also drawn the attention of policymakers worried about the huge trade deficit the United States is running with East Asia, particularly Japan, and its implications for American industry and workers.

But the attention of policymakers needs to be drawn to another challenge: the consequences for American strategic interests of a new Soviet policy toward the Far East. This policy, which aims at establishing Moscow as an active participant in the life of the region, raises a host of issues for the United States. Perhaps the most important of these is the future of the U.S.-Soviet-Chinese strategic triangle. A rapprochement between the latter two could have serious consequences for the global military balance sheet. Similarly, a rapprochement between the Soviet Union and Japan, encouraged perhaps by growing protectionist sentiments in the United States, could erode a critical American alliance.

The Far East is not unknown terrain for the Fund. In fact, its contributions to policy debate in this area include Gunnar Myrdal's epic *Asian Drama* along with Ralph N. Clough's *Island China.* But in recent years, other regions have captured its attention and resources. Robert A. Manning's proposal for this paper convinced us that once again the Fund could make a contribution in this area. A recognized expert on Asia, Manning, former Washington correspondent for the *Far Eastern Economic Review* and former diplomatic correspondent for *U.S. News & World Report,* has written extensively on U.S. security interests in the Pacific.

In the following pages, he traces, with great skill and insight, the ramifications for U.S. policy of Soviet initiatives. Underlying his analysis is the assumption that these initiatives not only present an opportunity for the United States to redefine its current posture in East Asia—which is now based on a loose, informal network of bilateral alliances, a quasi-alliance with China, and the now-eroded ANZUS alliance—but also provide the opportunity for greater superpower cooperation in the region. Mr. Manning has rekindled our interest in the Far East, and we are grateful to him for it.

Marcia Bystryn, ACTING DIRECTOR
The Twentieth Century Fund
November 1988

Contents

Introduction

Gorbachev and Asia

Soviet General Secretary Mikhail Gorbachev has dazzled the world and captured the public imagination, projecting an image of a new and different Soviet Union with potentially far-reaching consequences for the future of East-West relations. In stark contrast to the old stereotype of the grim, stone-faced, aging Bolshevik, the stylish, dynamic Gorbachev and his fashionable wife, Raisa, have become almost instant pop culture icons. One media-oriented political gesture after another has garnered the Communist leader unprecedented coverage as well as favorable ratings in public opinion polls in Europe and the United States. Gorbachev's book *Perestroika,* in which he uses a conversational tone to present his views, not only hit *The New York Times* best-seller list, but was just as avidly scooped off bookshelves in Beijing, Paris, and Bonn.

But if Mikhail Gorbachev has overnight changed popular perceptions of the Soviet Union, his steady stream of bold initiatives, unorthodox gestures, and speeches has generated a troublesome lack of consensus among Western Soviet-watchers and policymakers. Where previous Soviet leaders left the negotiating table over the U.S. "double zero" proposal to eliminate intermediate-range nuclear missiles, Gorbachev left Washington with no choice but to take "yes" for an answer. Where his predecessors vehemently opposed the Strategic Defense Initiative (SDI, or "Star Wars") and spared no effort to modernize their nuclear arsenal, Gorbachev softened the anti-Star Wars campaign, putting a startling 50 percent arms reduction accord within reach of the United States and the USSR. And where his predecessors attempted to relentlessly expand Soviet influence in the Third World, Gorbachev withdraws Soviet troops from Afghanistan and prepares to abandon its Marxist client regime. He has gone as far as to call Afghanistan Moscow's most ghastly transgression, a "bleeding wound."

Few dispute that Gorbachev is a different type of Soviet leader, that he is sincere, or that he seeks sweeping changes of an ossified Soviet system. No less a foe than Ronald Reagan has suggested that Moscow may have abandoned the goal of global domination. But have Soviet intentions really changed? Does Moscow seek a different role in the world? Is the nature of U.S.-Soviet relations changing?

An assessment of the Soviet Union under Gorbachev is hardly an academic exercise. An appraisal of current and prospective Soviet domestic policy and the foreign policy extended from it is one of the principal factors that will determine U.S. national security policy into the twenty-first century. Some analysts dismiss Gorbachev's policies and behavior as little more than a new veneer on Brezhnev-era policies and behavior. Others acknowledge his initiatives but argue that Gorbachev will succumb to domestic opponents and suffer the same ignominious fate as previous reformer Nikita Khrushchev. Another school of thought concedes that there is "new Soviet thinking" but that it has yet to be seen in new Soviet behavior. Another school argues that the new, less confrontational Soviet agenda is a temporary respite to recoup from the overextended adventurism of the 1970s and allow Gorbachev to revitalize and modernize the Soviet system. Finally, some experts believe that the restructuring of the Soviet system is sweeping and will endure, changing the political character of the Soviet Union, and its role in the world.

Gorbachev: The Asia Dimension

The ongoing debate about Gorbachev focuses almost exclusively on the meaning of Soviet policy for the West (especially for NATO), with little attention given to the Asia dimension. In heralding the coming "Pacific century," virtually all discussion about the Pacific Basin has systematically excluded the Soviet Union. Yet the Soviet Union is a Eurasian power; more than two-thirds of the USSR lies in Asia, and one-third of the Asian mainland is within Soviet borders. A distance of three miles between the Soviet island of Big Diomede and Alaska's Little Diomede separates the superpowers in the Pacific (see map, Appendix A).

Such ambiguity is not new. As Dostoyevsky observed a century ago, Russians tend to be regarded as Europeans in Asia and as Asiatics in Europe. Indeed, the story of Soviet Asia policy begins with the historic reality of a state condemned by geography to be a Eurasian nation. Preoccupation with establishing secure Asian frontiers, mixed with opportunistic desires to expand the contours of empire, has been a central theme in Soviet foreign policy from czarist times to the present. Ideology has influenced Soviet views of Asia, but it has not altered the basic geopolitical imperative that determines Soviet behavior toward the region.

The consequences of World War II, however, both heightened Soviet concerns with its Asian frontiers and created new opportunities to consolidate expansion. As one historian has written, "The wartime relocation of industries to Siberia, the invasion and occupation of Manchuria and northern Korea, and the acquisition of southern Sakhalin and the Kurile islands all gave the Soviet Union a greater stake in Northeast Asia by 1945."[1] In the aftermath of Moscow's confrontation by the German-Japan axis, Asia became increasingly bound up with Joseph Stalin's chief concern of securing European borders to maximum Soviet advantage.

The Soviet Union today is inextricably part of both the European and Asian strategic equation—geopolitical configurations that are increasingly intertwined. As we approach the twenty-first century, a new multipolar global power equation is taking shape. Four of the five poles in this emerging power structure—China, Japan, the United States, and the USSR—are Pacific powers, facing one another in Northeast Asia. When Undersecretary of State Lawrence Eagleburger commented in 1983 that there has been a "shift in the center of gravity of American foreign policy from the transatlantic relationship toward the Pacific Basin," it sent shock waves across Europe. The world is now beginning to adjust to this new reality.

Gorbachev has recognized this historic shift. Asia, he has written, "is the area where world politics will focus in the next century."[2] It is an area where Soviet policies are focusing even now. The Pacific has quickly become a top Soviet priority. While Europe is still first in its strategic calculus (Gorbachev speaks of Europe as the "common home"), Asia now runs a close second. Gorbachev's landmark Vladivostok speech in July 1986 was a dramatic demarche aimed at reclaiming Moscow's legitimacy as a Pacific power and defining a new Soviet agenda for Asia.

Gorbachev's new approach to the region promises to alter the geopolitics of East Asia, where bitter and often armed conflict among Communist powers (the USSR, China, Vietnam) has been a central political fact for the past two decades. The introduction of the "Gorbachev factor" is one of several new elements that will have a dramatic impact on U.S. interests and policies in Asia. The U.S. response to the Soviet initiative will be key in shaping Moscow's role as a Pacific power and in shaping the contours of the multipolar powers of the Pacific century.

• 1 •
The United States
and East Asia

Asia is the region where U.S. foreign policy has perhaps been most successful during the Reagan years. But suddenly many of the factors that made U.S. policy so effective in the 1980s are rapidly changing, creating complex new challenges for our Asia policy and rendering its future increasingly precarious.

Growing protectionist sentiment in the United States threatens the prosperity that once seemed unlimited in Asia. Conflicts and confrontation between the Communist states in East Asia (which served to strengthen the U.S. role) are beginning to dissipate. China and Japan are emerging as major powers. Burgeoning nationalism and antinuclear activism in the Pacific threaten to erode the U.S. patchwork alliance system in the region. And amidst all this flux a new Soviet approach to the Pacific Basin is complicating the political environment, altering threat perceptions among U.S. friends and allies in the region and changing the way the superpowers interact.

Failure to grasp unfolding trends and reluctance to fashion an activist response have been part of the historic pattern of American behavior toward Asia. It has resulted in wild swings in U.S. policy, from near isolationism to intense involvement in major military conflicts. The U.S. failure to understand where Japanese imperial expansion in the 1930s was leading contributed to the abrupt plunge into war in the Pacific. By defining Korea as outside the U.S. defense perimeter, the Truman administration inadvertently made the Korean War more likely. And by the time tens of thousands of U.S. troops were sent to Vietnam in the mid-1960s, the Sino-Soviet Communist monolith that was the underlying *raison d'etre* for U.S. intervention had been shattered for several years.

The consistent thread in U.S. policy has been an emphasis on maintaining a balance of power in Asia to prevent the rise of any hegemonic

5

force. This approach underpins other constant U.S. concerns: pursuit of commercial interests, free access to the region, and protection of the sea-lanes of communication (SLOCs). U.S. enforcement of a balance of power has helped underwrite stability in the Pacific since World War II, and is likely to be a major determinant of the region's stability for the foreseeable future.

If the United States is to sustain its own predominant position, however, it must begin to fathom the new dynamics of East Asia and adjust American policy accordingly. Despite the ascendant global role of the Pacific, American culture and history still nourish the view that our transatlantic ties lie at the heart of our national identity as a global power. The central foreign policy debates—over arms control, burden sharing, indeed, East-West relations—focus on Europe.

Yet it has become increasingly evident that Asia is playing the pivotal role in shaping America's future. From Japanese investment capital, bankrolling our mammoth budget deficits and buying our office buildings, to the thousands of Korean Hyundais filling our highways, few would dispute that the Pacific Basin already outstrips Europe in economic importance to the United States. U.S. trade with the Pacific Rim nations jumped to $238 billion in 1987, compared with $142 billion in trade with the EEC.[1] Between them, the United States and Japan account for some 35 percent of global gross national product (GNP), 55 percent of world banking assets,[2] and are both on the cutting edge of technologies (fiber optics, artificial intelligence, superconductivity) that will mold the world of the twenty-first century.

The countries of East Asia are a phenomenal economic success story. (See Table 1.) Between 1963 and 1985, Japan grew by an average of 5.9 percent a year, Hong Kong by 8.5 percent, South Korea by 8.7 percent, Taiwan by 9.2 percent, and Singapore by 9.5 percent.[3] Just as Japan has surpassed the Soviet Union to become the second-largest industrial economy, the newly industrialized "four dragons"—South Korea, Hong Kong, Singapore, and Taiwan—now threaten to become the next Japan. And China, which has averaged 10 percent annual growth since 1978, may become the world's fourth-largest economy by 2050, according to some estimates.

The notion of the "Pacific Century" is in large measure the result of the remarkable economic and financial integration of the region:

- Annual U.S.-Japan trade totals $120 billion
- The United States and Japan account for 70 percent of total foreign

Table 1

U.S. Trade with Key East Asian and Pacific (EAP) Countries: 1986–88 (in millions of dollars)

Country	U.S. Exports[a] (F.A.S.)				U.S. Imports (C.I.F.)			
	1986	1987	Jan–Apr 1987	Jan–Apr 1988	1986	1987	Jan–Apr 1987	Jan–Apr 1988
Indonesia	945.9	767.3	228.4	361.7	3,675.4	3,719.0	1,164.7	1,111.0
Malaysia	1,729.6	1,896.5	520.0	702.7	2,534.2	3,053.4	930.9	1,160.6
Philippines	1,363.3	1,599.0	492.4	593.6	2,150.3	2,481.1	713.6	898.8
Singapore	3,380.3	4,052.7	1,274.8	1,716.4	4,884.4	6,395.0	1,854.1	2,455.1
Thailand	936.1	1,544.0	352.9	540.6	1,872.6	2,387.1	713.9	1,030.6
ASEAN[b]	8,355.2	9,859.5	2,868.5	3,915.0	15,116.9	18,035.6	5,377.2	6,656.1
Australia	5,551.2	5,494.8	1,681.6	1,838.9	2,872.6	3,287.1	1,004.8	1,370.8
China	3,106.2	3,497.3	1,073.1	1,482.5	5,240.5	6,910.5	2,242.6	2,605.4
Hong Kong	3,030.1	3,983.1	1,199.9	1,629.4	9,473.6	10,490.2	2,935.4	3,027.7
Japan	26,881.6	28,248.6	8,129.2	11,853.3	84,456.7	88,073.8	27,447.9	29,311.8
Macao	2.7	5.4	1.1	1.1	444.5	548.7	150.0	157.2
New Zealand	880.8	818.5	243.3	251.1	1,097.4	1,180.4	380.7	488.1
South Korea	6,354.9	8,098.7	2,463.7	3,481.3	13,497.0	17,991.0	5,075.8	6,411.7
Taiwan	5,524.2	7,412.7	2,003.0	4,505.9[d]	21,251.5	26,406.5	8,019.2	8,282.3
EAP Total[c]	51,331.7	57,559.1	19,663.4	28,958.4	138,333.8	154,888.2	52,633.6	58,311.1
World Total	226,808.1	252,865.8	78,713.0	102,755.3	382,963.8	424,082.3	130,995.7	146,589.3

Source: U.S. Department of Commerce, Bureau of the Census. Compiled by Gary D. Bouck, Office of Pacific Basin.
a. Includes special category commodities, if any. b. Does not include Brunei, for which no 1988 figures are yet available. c. EAP total includes only 13 countries listed above. d. Figure includes $1,079.7 million in gold bullion for the Jan–Mar 1988 period.

investment in the states of ASEAN, the Association of Southeast Asian Nations (Thailand, Indonesia, Malaysia, the Philippines, Singapore, and Brunei)

- ASEAN is Washington's fifth-largest trading partner
- Inter-Pacific trade accounts for about half the total amount of trade in the Pacific Basin nations
- More than one-third of the exports of South Korea, Taiwan, Hong Kong, and Singapore are absorbed by the United States

This pan-Pacific economic integration is accompanied by the growing numbers and prominence of Asian-Americans, and confirmed by the tens of thousands of Asian students studying in the United States. In a sense, they are fostering what might be termed the "Pacific-ization of America."

The economic stakes reinforce East Asia's global strategic importance. The United States has six of its nine formal overseas treaty commitments (Japan, South Korea, the Philippines, Thailand, ANZUS [Australia, New Zealand, and the United States], and Micronesia) in this region, where it has fought three wars in the past forty-five years. The U.S. military partnership with Japan and quasi-alliance with China are central to U.S. efforts to contain Soviet global power as well as to the stability of the Pacific.

Recent U.S. Experience in Asia

For the Reagan administration, East Asia was an area of remarkably successful activism. After a shaky start, the administration managed to deepen institutional ties with China, integrate Beijing into the global economic system, and reduce the strategic component and fashion a more balanced relationship.[4] At the same time, Sino-American policy coordination on regional issues such as Afghanistan and Cambodia have succeeded in curbing Soviet influence, though such security collaboration has fallen far short of the overly optimistic expectations of many prominent analysts.[5]

The most dramatic change under President Reagan has been a decided tilt toward Japan as the cornerstone of U.S. strategy in the Asia/Pacific region. From a relatively passive client thriving under the U.S. security umbrella, Japan has shed its postwar pacifism and has dramatically improved its defense capabilities. This is in part a result of U.S. pressure, and in part a product of its emergence as a global power. It has taken on new roles and missions to defend adjacent areas in close military coordination with the United States. Tokyo's defense spending increased by more than 5 percent a year throughout the 1980s—its 1988 defense budget of $30 billion is the third largest in the world.[6]

Aside from enhancing its own defense forces, Japan has facilitated new U.S. conventional and nuclear deployments, enabling the modernization of U.S. forces within the Pacific Command. The modernization includes two squadrons of F-16s based at Misawa, Tomahawk cruise missiles based at Yokasuka, and two additional U.S. carrier battle groups. Tokyo has permitted—and largely financed—the new U.S. deployments of F-16 fighter jets and Tomahawk cruise missiles. These developments, which began to unfold under the Carter administration, have created a formidable *de facto* entente of the United States, China, and Japan—the first time in history these three powers have been aligned.

In addition, the United States has to a large extent solidified its relations with the ASEAN states. The administration, aided by large amounts of good luck, successfully helped manage democratic transitions in the Philippines and South Korea as both nations discarded authoritarian regimes. (The U.S. response to these events unexpectedly emphasized human rights, the same policy many Reagan officials had earlier criticized as one of the hallmarks of Carter's foreign policy.)

But this reassertion of American power, influence, and credibility in the Pacific over the past decade should not be taken for granted. The impermanence of the U.S. posture in Asia becomes readily apparent when it is contrasted with the predicament that existed only a decade previously in the Vietnam era.

In the aftermath of Vietnam, U.S. credibility and commitment—in Asia and more generally—were called into question. President Nixon's 1969 "Guam Doctrine," which called on Asian allies to become more self-reliant (and led to "Vietnamization" of the war) fueled perceptions of an eroding American commitment in the region. U.S. postwar alliance systems—the Southeast Asia Treaty Organization (SEATO), Central Treaty Organization (CENTO), and more recently, ANZUS—all came undone. The oil crisis of 1973–74 further contributed to the perception of declining American power.

As the United States was departing from Indochina, discredited and demoralized, Moscow was demonstrating an unprecedented assertiveness, supporting Third World leftists in such far-flung corners of the world as Angola, Ethiopia, and South Yemen. There was a sense of American drift. The 1977 decision to remove U.S. troops from Korea (subsequently reversed), the derecognition of Taiwan, and the fall of the Shah of Iran all reinforced a widespread perception that the United States was retrenching.

In fact, the seeds of the resurgent U.S. posture in Asia were planted even as Washington appeared to be retreating. It was the dramatic realignment of China in the early 1970s that facilitated the U.S. withdrawal from Vietnam and was the critical factor in rearranging the global balance of power. The Nixon-Kissinger opening to China allowed the United States to move from a two-and-a-half war strategy to a one-and-a-half war strategy. For Moscow, it meant preparing simultaneously for a two-front conflict in Europe and Asia, evoking fears of what historians dubbed the "1941 complex."

The Soviet Buildup

There is a symbiotic relationship between the strengthening of the U.S. alliance network in the Pacific over the past decade and Soviet behavior. It was Soviet threats against China that created one of the most significant geopolitical shifts of this century.[7] As Sino-Soviet hostilities increased in the mid-1970s, a cycle of action-reaction characterized a buildup in the region by both superpowers. (See Tables 2 and 3.)

Moscow's fears of an adverse shift in the "correlation of forces" led to a substantial Soviet buildup aimed at countering the United States and Japan in Northeast Asia, as well as containing China to the south. At the end of 1978, a new autonomous high command was put in charge of the Far East theater, reportedly with three subdivisions, responsible for the Far Eastern, Siberian, and Transbaikal military districts and Soviet forces in Mongolia. The Soviets rapidly modernized their forces and embarked upon substantial new deployments of air and seapower in this region, including a major expansion of their Pacific fleet.[8]

The accumulation of Soviet hardware in Asia since the 1978 phase began is impressive. There are now fifty-seven tank and motorized infantry divisions—about one-fourth of Soviet ground forces—numbering some 500,000 troops. Major military complexes were established at Vladivostok and Petropavlovsk. About one-fourth of the Soviet Air Force, some 2200 combat aircraft, are stationed in the Far East. But the most dramatic development is the Soviet naval presence: its Pacific fleet has grown from a coastal defense force into the largest of the four Soviet fleets, with some 90 surface combatants, 135 submarines, 2 Kiev-class carriers, 3 Kara-class guided missile antisubmarine warfare cruisers, Rogov-class transport ships providing amphibious capabilities, and a naval infantry division.[9]

The quality of Soviet forces improved along with the quantity, as Moscow deployed state-of-the-art military technology. This included T-72 tanks, Mig-27 Flogger fighters, Mig-29 Fulcrum interceptors, the Mig-31 Foxbat, and the Bear G and H models with new AS-15 air-launched cruise missiles (ALCMs).[10]

Another facet of this buildup was the deployment of theater and strategic nuclear systems. The Backfire medium-range bomber and SS-20 missiles were arrayed against China and Japan (and U.S. forces in Japan). In addition, SSN8 and SSN18 submarine-launched ballistic missiles (SLBMs) made it possible to target the United States without leaving the Soviet waters of the Sea of Okhotsk. This buildup, in turn, led to a new mission for Soviet conventional forces—protecting this "bastion" area bordering Japan. It is estimated that more than 35 percent of Soviet ICBMs and 30 percent of its strategic bombers are deployed east of the Urals.[11]

Accompanying this increase in Soviet military capabilities in Asia was a series of politically significant forward deployments. The 1979 Soviet

Table 2
U.S. Economic and Military Assistance, 1946–85
(in millions of dollars)

	Total Assistance Loans and Grants	Military Loans	Military Grants
Australia	123.6	115.6	—
Burma	272.7	—	89.4
Indochina	1,557.1	—	731.5
Indonesia	3,941.6	329.2	290.7
Japan	3,950.8	34.8	1,204.9
Kampuchea (Cambodia)	2,194.1	—	1,280.3
Laos	2,510.8	—	1,606.7
Malaysia	282.3	180.9	9.2
New Zealand	8.6	1.5	2.8
Pacific Is. Trust Terr.	824.2	—	—
Philippines	4,022.5	359.1	941.7
Singapore	22.1	17.2	2.1
South Korea	14,679.8	2,185.9	6,437.4
Taiwan	6,567.3	547.7	3,812.7
Thailand	2,412.1	563.2	1,537.0
Viet Nam	23,364.0	—	16,416.1

Source: U.S. AID, Department of Defense.

Table 3
Major Soviet Far East Forces, 1968–86

	1968	1973	1978	1981	1985	1986
Ground division	25+	40+	43	45+	53	57
Ships total	660	646	726	720	803	836
Carriers	0	0	0	1	2	2
Surface Combatants	55	60	67	80	81	84
Submarines						
(General purpose)	95	90	90	99	90	95
Submarines						
(SSN-SSBN)	10	20	30	30	32	25
Amphibs (LPD/LST)	0	4	9	11	14	14
Mine War (Ships/Craft)	110	115	110	95	95	105
Log-Spt-Misc[a]	390	357	420	404	485	510
Tactical Aircraft	1,050	1,370	1,405	1,355[c]	1,815[d]	1,860
(Fighter/Attack						
and Interceptors)						
Bombers	215	220	240	255	263[c]	250
			(LRA-175)	(LRA-150)	(SAF-155[c])	150
			(SNA-90)	(SNA-115)	(SNA-108[c])	100
ASW-Patrol	65	125	120	130(1)	154	170
SS-20 IRBM				75	162	147
Personnel total						
(in thousands)	[b]	610	679	701	813[c]	882
Army	210	380	410	430	530	570
Navy	105	115	119	121	143	159
Air Force	[b]	115	150[c]	150[c]	153	153
			(Includes Air Defense Forces)	(Includes Air Defense Forces)	(Includes Air Defense Forces)	

Source: U.S. Department of Defense

a. Includes patrol combatants, amphibious warfare craft, coastal patrol/river-roadstead craft, underway replenishment ships, material support ships, fleet support ships, and other auxiliaries b. Not available c. Approximate d. Excludes Strategic Defense Interceptors invasion of Afghanistan was the first large-scale, direct application of Soviet forces outside the Warsaw Pact. The establishment of Soviet bases in Vietnam marked the first full-scale, overseas Soviet facilities. Moscow deployed a full division of troops and two squadrons of Mig-23s on two of the northern islands that Japan lays claim to, and it increased its troop deployments in Mongolia to five divisions.

This muscular, blustering Soviet approach to Asia generated widespread fears throughout the region and fed a climate of confrontation that saw the decidedly un-Marxist spectacle of Communist states in East Asia in both direct confrontation and proxy clashes in Indochina. The turbulence in the region and perceptions of an enhanced Soviet menace helped solidify the U.S. alliance network in Asia.

The Asian Difference

But even under the most favorable circumstances, U.S. policy in Asia rests on a fragile set of relationships. The China tilt is but the most dramatic reminder that East Asia has been a region of shifting alignments. The core of Pacific security has been the U.S. forward deployment network that stretches from Japan, South Korea, and the Philippines to the atoll of Diego Garcia in the Indian Ocean, and on to the Persian Gulf (Oman and Saudi Arabia) and East Africa (Kenya and Somalia).

This vast region falls under the responsibility of the Pacific Command (PACOM). Managing the Pacific alliances is a daunting task, far more complex than its counterpart in the Atlantic. Unlike Europe, America's posture in Asia is based on a loose network of primarily bilateral alliances (that is, Japan, South Korea, the Philippines, individual ASEAN states, and Australia, as ANZUS is now in *de facto* suspension) and informal understandings with China, Taiwan, and states in Southeast Asia. In practice, CINCPAC (Commander-in-Chief, Pacific) is the functional equivalent of NATO's joint command.

Unlike NATO, the United States has no integrated command or multinational organization in the Pacific. Nor is there any regionwide grouping comparable to the European Community. As Seizaboro Sato and Henry Kissinger have pointed out, in Europe there is a multilateral alliance system, generally coordinated diplomacy, and a common history and culture on both sides of the Atlantic.[12] In Europe, there is also a clear, geographically contiguous dividing line separating rival blocs and a buffer area between Moscow and the West. However divergent the views about Soviet intentions and the degree of danger, there remains a shared Western perception of a common threat.

In Asia, none of these circumstances is present. For the United States, the Pacific is primarily a maritime and conventional theater where U.S. forces counter what are primarily Soviet land-based forces in Siberia and the Far East. Beyond these asymmetries, the Communist states have no Warsaw Pact. (Quite the contrary, they have been bitter rivals engaged in bloody conflict.) While in Europe political borders are mutually sanctified by the Helsinki accords, in East Asia there are not only a host of outstanding territorial claims (such as those between Japan and the USSR, China and Vietnam, over disputed islands) but basic questions of legitimacy and recognition between China and Taiwan, and North and South Korea.

Moreover, instead of the view of a common Soviet threat, there is a multiplicity of threat perceptions reflecting the diverse culture, history, and geography of the region. For example, some ASEAN states view Vietnam, not the Soviets, as the prime threat. Others, such as Indonesia and Malaysia, consider it to be China. The two Koreas view each other and Japan as key threats, and China increasingly sees Japan as a rival and potential threat. The lines of conflict are East-East as well as East-West.

None of these nations however (with the exception of North Korea) views the United States as a threat. Rather, Washington is relied upon as the security bridge, buffer, and guarantor of the balance of power. It is the United States that links the otherwise inchoate members in a loose coalition. Though the ostensible mission of the U.S. presence is to deter the Soviet threat, Washington also plays an important (unstated and largely unacknowledged) auxiliary role: mitigating fears of real and potential inter-Asian conflict. In essence, PACOM's most important peacetime function may be neither military nor strategic, but psychological and political.

With the United States safely an ocean away, the American presence in the region is reassuring. It is a peculiar presence, serving at once as enforcer to deter potential aggressors, honest broker, and partner. Paradoxically, this comforting security blanket role is likely to become more important in the near future with the emergence of regional powers such as China and Japan, and as decreasing perceptions of a Soviet threat erode the stated rationale of the U.S. presence. A reduced Soviet threat, however, will not necessarily mean less instability, and the critical factor shaping the geopolitical balance in Asia will likely be—in the future as in the past—a credible American presence.

How to maintain that balance of power in the 1990s is one of the prime challenges confronting U.S. interests in Asia.

The paradox is that even as nationalist pressures render future U.S. military presence in South Korea or the Philippines uncertain, no other country is able to play the U.S. counterbalancing role without threatening the stability of the region. Neither China nor Japan nor the Soviet Union would be acceptable substitutes to others in the region. While the United States could maintain sufficient forward deployment capabilities by moving its bases to U.S.-controlled territory (that is, Guam, Saipan, Tinian, Palau), any new arrangement that was percieved as an American reluctance to continue its role as guarantor could upset the balance of power.

The current trendy debate over the extent of U.S. overseas commitments (see Table 4) and the need for more allied burden sharing is epitomized

Table 4
U.S. Active-Duty Military Personnel Strengths: Positioning of Forces

Regional Area/Country	Total
East Asia and Pacific	
Australia	746
Japan	48,104
Philippines	16,068
South Korea	43,113
Thailand	146
Other	246
Afloat	20,180
TOTAL	128,623
U.S. Territory and Special Locations	
Continental U.S., Puerto Rico, and Virgin Islands	1,475,055
Alaska	20,777
Hawaii	46,122
Guam	8,989
Johnston Atoll	150
Other	92
Afloat	168,808
TOTAL	1,719,993
All Foreign Countries	
Ashore	453,664
Afloat	71,640
TOTAL	525,304
Total Worldwide	
Ashore	1,928,719
Afloat	240,393
TOTAL	2,169,112

Source: U.S. Department of Defense.

by the remarkable success of Paul Kennedy's book *The Rise and Fall of the Great Powers*. The domestic discussion of alleged U.S. decline and new global realities underscores the internal pressures on U.S. policy makers, while the perception of American retreat abroad erodes U.S. credibility among its allies. Clearly, it will be difficult to manage the devolution from a bipolar world to one in which both superpowers have reduced clout, where their respective arsenals yield increasingly less political influence, and where the web of interdependency demands new rules of the game.

New Trends: Approaching the 1990s

At present, the United States is still the leading actor on the Pacific stage, but the arena is now hosting a very different political, economic, and strategic drama than in the past. East Asia is a region in ferment and transition. A broad trend toward democratic processes is occurring amidst difficult generational leadership changes facing both Confucian/authoritarian and Leninist regimes.

The economic success of Japan and the East Asian newly industrialized countries (NICs) has spawned a new set of problems. The centrifugal forces of the global economy are transcending ideological and political boundaries, leaping ahead of political institutions that are not prepared to absorb the economic shifts. Taiwan and South Korea, both vehemently anti-Communist, are engaged in booming trade and investment with China and the Soviet bloc. At the same time, protectionist rumblings and trade friction abound, threatening to impede economic growth and disrupt the region's cohesiveness. There is a growing antinuclear movement in the South Pacific, which has already led to New Zealand's suspension from ANZUS and now clouds U.S. negotiations with the Philippines over the future of Clark Air Base and Subic Bay Naval Station, the two largest overseas U.S. bases, where current agreements expire in 1991.

Geopolitical currents are also shifting. Conflicts between Communist states are easing. With China (PRC) and the Soviet Union moving toward a climate of detente, the configuration of the U.S.-USSR-PRC strategic triangle is altered. China is increasingly asserting itself: its sales of Silkworm missiles to Iran, intermediate-range missiles to Saudi Arabia, and its conflict with Vietnam over the widely contested Spratly Islands testify to Beijing's newfound independence. Steady movement toward a settlement of the Cambodia (Kampuchea) conflict and an end to Hanoi's occupation of that tragic land promises to redraw the political landscape of Southeast Asia. The continuing Communist insurgency in the Philippines and growing Philippine nationalism may further alter alignments in the region. And tension between Beijing and Tokyo, the two primary Asian powers, may be a harbinger of regional nationalisms in conflict.

The nations of East Asia are at differing stages of uncertain political transitions that are occurring as economic modernization is fostering new pressures to transform both authoritarian and Leninist systems. The stunning "People Power" revolt that swept away the Marcos dictatorship and restored democratic institutions to the Philippines in 1986 has catalyzed a regionwide trend. South Korea and Taiwan are undergoing processes of democratization; aging leaders in China, North Korea, Vietnam, Indonesia, Burma, and Singapore are beginning to yield power to a new generation. (See Table 5.)

In broad terms, the trend toward democracy is clearly favorable to U.S. interests, tending to discredit statist models and to favor market-oriented and more popularly based systems. But democratization is part of a greater economic and political independence that also reflects a deepening sense of nationalism with the potential to change regional alignments. For example, where the United States could quietly negotiate base accords with Marcos, the new Philippine constitution requires an agreement to be in the form of a treaty ratified by its congress, which

Table 5
Senior [a] Political Leaders in Asia

Government	Leader[b]	Age in 1987	Years in continuous power
Burma	Ne Win*	76	25
China	Deng Xiaoping	83	10
Indonesia	Suharto	66	21
North Korea	Kim Il Sung	75	39
Singapore	Lee Kuan Yew	63	28[c]
Sri Lanka	Junius Richard Jayewardene	80	9
Taiwan	Chiang Ching-kuo**	77	11

Source: East-West Center, Honolulu: University of Hawaii
* Resigned in July 1988 ** Died in early 1988
a. Based on age or years in power. b. Based on effective importance in policymaking, not necessarily formal position. c. Includes the periods when Singapore was a self-governing British colony and a state in Malaysia.

may also call a popular plebiscite. Similarly, where dictators like South Korea's Park Chung Hee might have been amenable to U.S. demands, Seoul's new President Roh Tae Woo, who was elected by a slim 36 percent plurality and governs with a minority in parliament, must pay careful heed to public opinion when dealing with Washington. Democracy in East Asia could alter U.S.-bilateral relations with several states.

This growing sense of national assertiveness is fueled by two other trends—distress over U.S. protectionist tendencies and an Asian perception of American decline, resulting in a sense of unease. The massive U.S. budget and trade deficits are widely viewed as symptoms of American malaise. In 1987, 62 percent of the U.S. trade deficit ($107 billion) resulted from trade with Pacific Rim countries.[13] Key allies are also becoming economic competitors. But the world trade regime lags behind the economic realities of the NICs' entry into advanced industrial and high-technology sectors, the absorption of centrally planned economies into the market system, and in mechanisms to resolve disputes over copyright, patent, and other intellectual property laws.

Evidence of the mutual frustration and mounting anger from these trade problems is strewn across the shores of both sides of the Pacific. In the United States, congressmen smash Toshiba radios on the steps of the Capitol, while in South Korea, farmers protest in front of the U.S. embassy in Seoul, and government-sanctioned unions in staunchly pro-American Singapore demonstrate against the removal of U.S. trade privileges. In Australia, conservative wheat farmers (irked at American farm subsidies) protest against joint electronic intelligence facilities. A bitter dispute in April 1987 over a copyright law engendered by U.S. pressure triggered the collapse of the Thai government, forcing new elections.

The dissipation of inter-Communist conflict is another indicator of a regional order in transition. The unfolding Sino-Soviet rapprochement will have political reverberations in East Asia and beyond. Increasing economic interaction between the Communist states and the market economies is likely to reduce traditional political antagonisms in the region. China and the Soviet Union compete for Western investment, and Vietnam and Cambodia may soon join the fold of ASEAN in Southeast Asia. These developments are rapidly altering the threat perceptions in East Asia, fears that the United States has traditionally mobilized to gain support for its national security policies.

These trends introduce a new element of uncertainty to prospects for regional stability, and to a number of assumptions underlying U.S. policy toward Asia. It is less U.S. decline than East Asian ascendancy that has generated new questions about U.S. global commitments. Nationalism in Korea and the Philippines suggests that a significant U.S. military presence in either country may not persist into the next century. Yet a forward-deployed U.S. military posture is likely to continue to be of major importance to regional stability. The anomaly of the world's biggest debtor (United States) serving as the security guarantor of the world's largest creditor (Japan) underscores the extent to which domestic matters have become foreign policy issues. It also highlights the dilemma of an erratically emerging multipolar world. The grace (or lack thereof) with which the United States manages the transitions to new security arrangements will be critical to the stability of any future alignments.

The most difficult new factor for the United States, however, is the Soviet Union. Over the past decade, aggressive Soviet behavior has served to mold a negative image and isolate Moscow in the Pacific. New Soviet overtures and a more conciliatory and benign-appearing approach is resulting in a sharp decline in the perception of the Soviet threat in much of Asia. As the active ingredient of alliances is fear, Soviet policy toward Asia may ultimately become an important factor in defining the fate and contours of the U.S. presence in the Pacific.

• 2 •
Enter Gorbachev:
Behind "New Thinking"

As Mikhail Gorbachev assumed the reins of power in March 1985, the Soviet Union, with its fourth leader in less than three years, had already begun to reassess its priorities, assumptions, and ideological conceptions. Asia was but one of an accumulation of domestic and foreign problems that attained crisis proportions. To a beleaguered Soviet elite, a dark shadow seemed to hover over the nation's future. Gorbachev himself explained that, by the latter part of the 1970s, "elements of what we call stagnation and other phenomena alien to socialism began to appear in the life of society."[1]

Moscow's New Priorities

This awareness produced Gorbachev's sweeping efforts to reform the Soviet system—perestroika (restructuring) and glasnost (openness). It also generated the ideas and assumptions underpinning an equally novel approach to foreign policy designed to facilitate Gorbachev's top priority—reinvigorating the economic and political system. Thus Moscow seeks to create a peaceful international environment, allowing it to maximize the resources available for Soviet economic modernization.

The main features of Gorbachev's still-emerging foreign policy are: strategic retreat, to gain a respite from the overextension wrought by Leonid Brezhnev's activism; projection of a more benign image in an effort to weaken U.S. alliance systems and to create a strategic environment more favorable to Soviet interests; replacement of millenial ideology with geopolitical national interest; drift away from a socialist economic bloc and toward an embrace of the world economic and financial system; a de-emphasis of Third World radicalism; and a growing Soviet political role in brokering international conflicts.

The changes in Soviet policy have been accompanied by a wholesale purge of personnel in the foreign policy apparatus. The International Department (ID) of the Communist party, responsible for formulating the theoretical guidelines underlying Soviet foreign policy, is now filled with a coterie of sophisticated "Americanists" led by Gorbachev confidant Aleksandr Yakovlev. Karen Brutents, a scholar with a lengthy record of deep skepticism about leftist regimes in the Third World, is now in charge of Third World affairs.[2] Parallel changes have occurred in the Soviet Ministry of Foreign Affairs.

The most demonstrable change has been a newfound adroitness in public relations skills. But there is far more to Moscow's new approach to foreign affairs than just style and tone. With increasing frequency, articles in the Soviet press condemn the failures of past Soviet foreign policy, attributing them to a mistaken tendency to use military force as a prime instrument for advancing foreign policy. In a recent *Izvestia* commentary, Aleksandr Bovin, a leading political analyst, chided Moscow's decisions to deploy SS-20 missiles in Europe and to send troops into Afghanistan as "typical examples" of this misguided approach, "geared to the use of strong-arm methods in foreign policy." In both cases, he argued, "we clearly overestimated our possibilities and underestimated what could be called the resistance of the environment."[3]

There are several key factors underlying this Soviet reappraisal: resource constraints and the need to modernize its techno-industrial base; a negative cost/benefit assessment of three decades of Soviet behavior in Asia, Africa, and Latin America; and a realization that Soviet adventurism in the 1970s undermined detente.

All of the new assumptions, priorities, and trends that characterize Gorbachev's foreign policy find expression in Soviet policy toward Asia. The emphasis on rehabilitating the Soviet economy has led to vigorous efforts by Moscow to lay a basis for connecting its economic future to the dynamic Pacific Basin. Essential to achieving this objective is the need to eradicate what Soviet analysts refer to as "the enemy image" left over from Brezhnev's approach to the region, and to foster a political environment where broader economic and technological cooperation can flourish.

What we have seen in Gorbachev's approach to Asia is a pattern of bold diplomatic demarches punctuated with Soviet concessions. Overtures toward China are underscored by concessions—on border issues, on Afghanistan, on troop withdrawals from Mongolia. Praise is lavished on Beijing's reforms, on Japan's economic success, on the importance of ASEAN. Myriad arms control proposals for Asia are prefaced by a Soviet commitment to destroy SS-20 missiles deployed in Asia as part of the INF treaty. Gorbachev's retreats—Afghanistan and the INF accords—provide political currency for a less intimidating style and innovative diplomacy that have begun to reshape perceptions and open new possibilities for Soviet foreign policy.

But Gorbachev's Asia policy must be viewed in the larger context of the overall reassessment of Soviet interests. Reappraisals did not originate with Gorbachev, but evolved toward the end of the Brezhnev era. They were evident in the writings of Soviet think-tank analysts by the early 1980s and began to percolate up to official levels from the start of the short-lived tenure of Yuri Andropov.[4] To grasp the course upon which Moscow is now headed, therefore, it is instructive to examine the process by which it developed.

From Brezhnev to Gorbachev

The revealing contrast between Brezhnev's report to the Twenty-sixth Party Congress in 1981 and the official statements of Andropov and Gorbachev illustrates the evolution of Soviet perceptions. Brezhnev devoted a large portion of the document to the Third World, enthusiastically trumpeting the "fresh victories" of the "revolutionary struggles of peoples" that were altering the "correlation of forces" in Moscow's direction. "No one should doubt," Brezhnev said, "the CPSU will continue to pursue consistently the development of cooperation between the USSR and the liberated countries. . . ."[5]

A spate of coups and anticolonial revolutions in the mid-1970s—in Angola, Mozambique, Ethiopia, South Yemen, and Afghanistan—brought to power a host of leftist regimes, all with varying degrees of Soviet assistance. This was part of a new wave of Soviet activism that served two important functions: First, it was part of the Soviet quest for strategic parity with the United States, expanding Soviet influence and demonstrating a global reach. Second, it masked domestic stagnation and provided some credibility for the Soviet leadership.

In retrospect, Brezhnev's adventurism appears the last gasp of the Bolshevik era. Expansionism in the Third World—the specter of the spread of socialism—in tandem with its Asian military buildup, did more than demonstrate that Moscow was undeniably a military superpower. It helped camouflage a petrified system—the Stalinist model—that was intellectually exhausted, economically untenable, and politically static. Worse still, it obstructed efforts to come to grips with Moscow's problems by essentially denying their existence.

This all began to change with the ascension of Yuri Andropov to secretary general. Andropov's overriding concern was domestic economic reform. He absorbed some of the burgeoning doubts reflected in the writings of the Soviet intelligentsia. In his first major statement on the Third World, the former KGB chief pointed to the accumulation of Third World clients as a burden, impinging on scarce Soviet resources. Speaking at a Central Committee plenum in June 1983, he said:

> Most close to us in the former colonial world are the countries which have chosen the socialist orientation. . . . We see, of course, the complexity of their position and the difficulties of their revolutionary development. It is one thing to proclaim socialism and quite another to build it. For this, a certain level of productive forces, culture and social consciousness are needed . . . we contribute also, to the extent of our ability, to their economic development. But on the whole, their economic development, just as the entire social progress of those countries can be only the result of the work of their peoples and a correct policy of their leadership.[6]

This remarkable statement hints at two key elements of the ongoing reappraisal: disillusionment with the spate of self-proclaimed Marxist regimes and the implication that Moscow might better contribute to world socialism by force of example. The tone of Andropov's speech is also striking. The cheerleading accolades to "national liberation movements" are replaced by a new sobriety.

Gorbachev went a step further. In his report to the Twenty-seventh Party Congress, he echoed Andropov, expressing lukewarm support for "socialist-oriented" states, cautioning that the USSR would provide aid "to the extent of its abilities" and that these nations should develop "mainly through their own efforts." The best help Moscow can provide, explained Gorbachev, is to be a shining example of socialism: "The CPSU sees as its main internationalist duty, the successful development of our country." But he did not even discuss the Third World, nor did he make any of the standard triumphant references to Soviet clients. For Gorbachev, the test of socialism is the success of the Soviet system itself.

It is not difficult to discern the underlying causes for this change in attitude. In the mid-1960s, there were only three countries in the Third World dubbed "Marxist-Leninist." A decade later, there were sixteen, with varying degrees of military and economic dependence on Moscow.

By 1981, twelve had friendship treaties with the Soviets, and according to a 1983 Rand study, the cost of Moscow's imperial burden mushroomed from about \$13.6 billion in 1971 to between \$35.9 and \$46.5 billion by 1981.[7] If Brezhnev proved that the Soviet Union was indeed a superpower, Gorbachev discovered that empire was expensive and a bit overrated.

The Gorbachev Doctrine

One striking feature of the policy direction thus far articulated by Gorbachev is a move away from ideology toward a more pragmatic approach, though still couched in Leninist jargon. Moscow is redefining itself more as a nation-state than a millenial cause. Rather than stressing rivalry between two competing economic systems, Gorbachev's "new thinking" stresses an enthusiastic embrace of global interdependence. Moscow has begun to float offerings in the Euromarket, establish ties with the EEC, pursue joint ventures with foreign firms, and is actively considering the possibility of a convertible ruble.[8]

Moscow appears to view greater association with the Western trade and financial systems as key to its technological and industrial future. It is expressing interest in affiliating itself with the IMF and the World Bank, which in the past were roundly denounced as instruments of capitalist exploitation. It is also seeking to join the General Agreement on Tariffs and Trade (GATT), and has already attained observer status in the Asian Development Bank (ADB).

To create a theoretical basis for his shift from the stance of conflict between competing social systems to a policy based on cooperation and interdependence, Gorbachev has tried to redefine the concept of peaceful coexistence. Since Lenin, the idea of peaceful coexistence has been based on the belief in the inevitable triumph of socialism over capitalism. But Gorbachev explains that modern conditions, such as the threat of nuclear disaster and the need to protect the environment, require a new interdependence that supersedes class conflict. "Security," he tells us, "is indivisible. It is either equal security for all or none at all."[9]

Thus, at the Twenty-seventh Party Congress, the idea that unceasing class conflict between two social systems was at the root of peaceful coexistence was dropped from the party program. Foreign Minister Eduard Shevardnadze affirmed this view most bluntly at a July 1988 Foreign Ministry conference, explaining, "The struggle between two opposing social systems is no longer a determining tendency of the present era." The coexistence of socialism and capitalism, we are now told, can be a permanent state of affairs.

But Yegor Ligachev, a high-ranking Politburo official, has cast doubt on that assertion. In the first public dissension from Gorbachev's foreign policy since his ascension to power, Ligachev said in a widely publicized August 5, 1988, speech at Gorki that foreign policy proceeds from "the class character of international relations. Any other way of putting this question introduces confusion into the consciousness of our people and our friends abroad." Moreover, Ligachev further challenged Gorbachev's central premise, arguing that "the struggle against the nuclear threat by no means signifies any artificial braking of the social and national liberation struggle."[10]

Ligachev's speech, part of a larger ongoing campaign to define an alternative version of perestroika, did not go unanswered. As Gorbachev was vacationing on the Black Sea, Aleksandr Yakovlev, his confidant and a Politburo member, gave equally publicized rebuttals to Ligachev the following week. "Common human interests . . . unite mankind, and that means they are capable of overcoming the forces of disunity, opposition, and confrontation." These values, Yakovlev concluded, "call for the renunciation of the dogmatic view of the world."[11] This debate at the highest levels of the Kremlin underscores the tentativeness of Gorbachev's "new thinking" on foreign policy.

Gorbachev's public posture toward the socialist countries also suggests a marked departure from that of his predecessors. Where Brezhnev forced political conformity at gunpoint, Gorbachev praises diversity. In a speech at the seventieth anniversary of the Bolshevik Revolution, Gorbachev derided the "arrogance of omniscience," and called for a "more sophisticated culture of mutual relations" among socialist states. "We have satisfied ourselves," he explained, "that unity does not mean identity and uniformity. We have become convinced of there being no 'model' of socialism to be emulated by everyone." A joint declaration signed during Gorbachev's March 1988 trip to Yugoslavia codifies these ideas, even citing the UN Charter provisions against the use of force.[12]

Such thoughts must make Brezhnev turn over in his grave. It was the Brezhnev Doctrine, brutally demonstrated in Moscow's 1968 invasion of Czechoslovakia, that set the standard for socialist conformity. It established that the Soviet Union maintains the right to intervene to enforce what it deems proper socialist policies if an allied Communist regime strays too far from the Kremlin line. It is difficult to escape the irony of Gorbachev now borrowing many of his market-oriented reforms from Eastern Europe, too difficult, in fact, for the wisecracking Soviet foreign affairs spokesman, Gennadi Gerasimov. When asked last year what the difference is between the then-intolerable reforms attempted by Czech leader Alexander Dubcek and those of Gorbachev today, he replied, "Nineteen years."

There is little question that the "Gorbachev Doctrine" allows far greater political latitude to Warsaw Pact states. It does not impose ideological rigor on Communist regimes—a new factor facilitating Sino-Soviet reconciliation. But this socialist pluralism, like most of Gorbachev's public positions, has yet to be tested. How would Moscow react if, say, Poland allowed independent trade unions? Or if Hungary or China permitted a multiparty system?

Gorbachev's response to the crisis in Poland, one of the first major tests of Moscow's tolerance, suggests that Moscow may allow in practice the pluralism it is preaching. In September, Moscow signaled its approval for the Polish regime to strike a deal legalizing the independent trade union, Solidarity. In a remarkable interview with *Le Monde,* Soviet Central Committee spokesman Nikolai Shishlin praised Warsaw's efforts "to involve all the forces in the country in their national renewal process" as "good evidence of realism, which we welcome." Shishlin went still further, stating, "We would not be afraid if Solidarity emerged . . . trade union pluralism is not heresy."[13]

Such comments, plus Kremlin decisions such as the one permitting massive demonstrations for more autonomy in the Baltic states (Estonia, Latvia, Lithuania), are an indication that the "Gorbachev Doctrine" may replace the Brezhnev Doctrine in deed as well as word.

Another feature of Gorbachev's "new look" foreign policy is a markedly different approach to the developing countries. Moscow has actively begun to cultivate the larger, geopolitically important Third World states such as India, Indonesia, the Philippines, Brazil, and Mexico. This is not an ad hoc policy, but part of a new conceptual framework based on the view that conflicts of interest between the United States and major capitalist-oriented developing states offer low-cost, low-risk opportunities for the Soviets to expand their influence and erode U.S. ties to its allies.

Amid widespread disillusion amongst Soviet theorists about the strategy of promoting leftist client states such as Angola, Ethiopia, Afghanistan, and South Yemen, key Gorbachev advisers Brutents and Yakovlev were among the few who had an alternative approach.[14] Brutents argued that such conflicts of interest provide "the solid base for the Soviet Union's cooperation with those liberated countries where capitalist relations are developing but which pursue a policy of defending and strengthening national sovereignty in politics and economics."[15] Yakovlev echoes Brutents in heralding "the appearance of sufficiently strong young capitalist states—the 'newly industrializing countries'—which are at the same time object and agent of economic expansion. They—for instance, Brazil, Mexico, and Argentina—have their own monopolistic groups, in certain cases capable of entering the struggle against the 'old' industrial empires."[16] This approach fits into a larger multipolar framework that Yakovlev views as having the potential for reducing U.S. global influence. "New centers of power have mushroomed up," he explains. "Europe and Japan have emerged."

This rationale propels bold new Soviet diplomatic initiatives—from the reflagging of the Kuwaiti tankers in the Persian Gulf to Foreign Minister Shevardnadze's trips to Latin America in 1986 and 1987. It is clearly behind a host of Soviet Asian gambits and explains why Gorbachev has renewed Moscow's traditional focus on India. Gorbachev met four times in two years with Indian Prime Minister Rajiv Gandhi, reaching accord on a host of economic and military aid programs.

The effort to expand Soviet influence and weaken U.S. alliances is reminiscent of Khrushchev's tactics. But there is one critical difference: Khrushchev regarded his overtures to newly independent states (Sukarno's Indonesia, Nehru's India, and U Nu's Burma) as promoting a "noncapitalist road" that would eventually lead developing nations to socialism; Gorbachev approaches them from a realpolitik view without either exaggerated optimism or ideological baggage.

The final new element in Soviet foreign policy under Gorbachev is the still vaguely defined concept of "reasonable sufficiency" in defense. This shift in Soviet military doctrine reduces Soviet military requirements, according to Defense Minister Dimitri Yazov, to "the magnitude of armed forces necessary to defend oneself against attack from outside."[17] This would permit massive reductions in conventional and nuclear forces, creating the strategic environment of "mutual security" often mentioned by Gorbachev. Michael McGwire, a military analyst at the Brookings Institution, has argued that this shift is the result of a series of changes in Soviet doctrine that actually began in the 1960s.[18] Despite its nebulousness, "reasonable sufficiency" was formally adopted as doctrine by the Warsaw Pact in a May 1987 declaration that denied "any aspiration to possess armed forces and arms in excess of what is necessary" to repel any aggression.[19]

The outward signs of change in the Soviet approach to military issues are striking. Take, for example, the spectacle of Soviet Chief of Staff

Marshal Sergei Akhromeyev having heart-to-hearts with his American counterpart, touring American military installations, and climbing into the cockpit of a B-1 bomber during an unprecedented July 1988 visit to the United States. An equally mind-boggling bit of military glasnost was Defense Secretary Frank Carlucci's tour the same month of the Kremlin's top-secret bases and inspection of their state-of-the-art fighter. Soviet officials have even hinted that they may begin publishing their defense budget.

But, appearances aside, changes in basic military doctrine are hardly assured. There is intense debate in the Soviet Union over the "reasonable sufficiency" concept: the Foreign Ministry and think tanks are its most ardent proponents, while the military establishment puts up substantial resistance.[20] Defense Minister Yazov, for example, wrote in a pamphlet distributed to thousands of Soviet officers in October 1988 that "it is impossible to rout an aggressor with defense alone," adding that the Red Army "must be able to conduct a decisive offensive" after repelling an attack.

A critical measure of the failure of the Soviet military to embrace "reasonable sufficiency" is the stark reality that there have been no changes in the size or organization of Soviet force structures. Gorbachev's flexibility—toward the INF treaty, toward a Strategic Arms Reduction Talks (START) agreement that would result in a 50 percent cut in nuclear forces, and toward an asymmetrical reduction in conventional forces in Europe—may be preliminary evidence that "reasonable sufficiency" is more than a rhetorical or propaganda device. The problem, as with other aspects of Gorbachev's "new thinking," is that there is still a sizable gap between the concept and actual Soviet behavior.

Whatever Gorbachev's intentions, implementation of his foreign policy vision is constrained by the Brezhnev legacy. The resulting bureaucratic inertia has impeded the realization of Gorbachev's policy and helps explain why Soviet behavior displays many areas of continuity. But Gorbachev, as the *Economist* recently pointed out, "has moved to new ground." To the extent that Moscow changes its behavior—that is, reduces its military profile, joins the world market—superpower competition may lose its ideological component and more closely resemble a nuclearized version of traditional great power rivalry.

The ambiguity of Soviet foreign policy is particularly noticeable in the case of Asia: Moscow has neither reduced its military posture nor (with the exception of Afghanistan) abandoned any of its commitments. Since 1985, the Soviets have added four divisions to their Far East forces, and the number of ships and submarines in the Pacific fleet has increased from 819 to 861. Similarly, aid to Vietnam and North Korea has increased, and the strategic relationship between Moscow and Pyongyang has been enhanced. If the Soviets have not embarked on any new adventures in the Third World since Afghanistan, it is also true that there has been a dearth of opportunities. In many cases, Moscow has kept its options open (for example, flirting with the Communist Party of the Philippines/New People's Army [CPP/NPA] in the Philippines). The continuity in Soviet behavior, then, presents an impediment to real political breakthroughs in Asia, but the prospect and promise of change have tended to mask the continuity.

Gorbachev, however, has created modest success in the region by reshaping perceptions. The combination of Soviet concessions, intrigue over the dramatic changes inside the Soviet Union, and his more flexible and accommodating diplomacy have had an effect. The less threatening image of the USSR increases U.S. vulnerability. The receptivity of China and ASEAN to Soviet overtures testifies to the new political environment Gorbachev is fostering in the Pacific.

Nonetheless, Gorbachev still has a problem in Asia. The achievement of the first phase of Moscow's new Asia policy is largely limited to gaining acceptance of the Soviet Union as a legitimate participant in the economic and political arena of the Pacific Basin. This is the requisite for a successful Soviet policy. For Gorbachev, the problem is what to do next. Further concessions—necessary to advance Soviet policy goals in Asia— will be substantially more difficult and politically riskier than those offered so far.

A political breakthrough with China, for example, would likely require a substantial drawdown of Soviet troops along the border and further territorial concessions, although Beijing would not sacrifice its relations with the West. Even more precarious would be a Soviet initiative toward Japan; for example, returning the Northern Territories claimed by Japan could affect the security of Soviet strategic forces in the Sea of Okhotsk. Is the Soviet internal political consensus in support of "new thinking" so broad that the military would accede to such moves, or do domestic constraints form the limits of Gorbachev's new Asia policy?

Still another area of uncertainty affecting key assumptions of Gorbachev's Asia policy is the fate of perestroika. The first stage of Soviet economic reforms has increased neither productivity nor hard currency earnings nor global competitiveness. Economic engagement in Asia and the Pacific hinges on success in these areas. Without it, Moscow's ability to export to and import from the Pacific Basin would be severely circumscribed. Regional expectations would dwindle, as would the underlying rationale for more active Soviet participation in the Pacific.

All these problems facing Gorbachev underscore the gap between rhetoric and reality, conception and implementation. In a blunt confession of the failures of perestroika, Gorbachev told Soviet editors on September 25, "We are going slowly . . . and this means we are losing the game. In a word it turns out here is a gap between our goals and our work."[21]

This sense of urgency to inject momentum into his reforms led to hastily convened sessions of the Central Committee and Supreme Soviet five days later. When the dust settled from the weekend sessions, the Soviets had a new Politburo and a completely restructured party and government apparatus. Gorbachev removed four members of the Politburo, reduced the influence of key conservative Politburo opponents Ligachev and Viktor Chebrikov (who lost his post as KGB chief), placed his protege Vadim Medvedev in charge of ideology, and put Yakovlev in charge of a party commission for foreign affairs. At the same time, the Soviet leader reorganized the party structure and was unanimously elected to a new executive post of president.

If these moves have the intended consequence of removing key impediments to perestroika, Gorbachev's foreign policy will rest on a firmer foundation. Nonetheless, in three years Gorbachev has set a new course for Soviet foreign policy in Asia and beyond. Close examination of the path his policy has followed thus far offers some clues as to how durable the policy is and how enduring the promised new Soviet global role may be.

• 3 •
From Vladivostok:
Gorbachev's Asia Gambit

It was a dazzling gesture in the now-familiar style of Mikhail Gorbachev: with one bold stroke, the Soviet leader sought in his benchmark July 28, 1986, Vladivostok speech to inject a new vitality into a stale and outmoded Soviet Asia policy (see Appendix B). It is a measure of Moscow's isolation that Gorbachev felt compelled to remind the world that "the Soviet Union is also an Asian and Pacific country."[1] In a belated recognition of the region's dynamism—a dynamism that Gorbachev wanted the Soviet Union to partake of—he prefaced his remarks with a plaintive discourse on the importance of Asia and the "bonds of interdependence" that "call us to look for ways to unify and establish open ties between nations within the region and beyond it."[2]

Gorbachev's initiative was a means of displaying the thrust of his "new thinking" in action, articulating a sharp departure from the Asian policy of his predecessors. But smoke and mirrors aside, what remains that is really new?

Clearly, Soviet policy toward Asia was ripe for a major overhaul. Brezhnev's counterproductive policies had left Moscow with diminishing credibility outside of its Communist client states (North Korea, Mongolia, Indochina). Its military buildup was the foundation of a blustering approach characterized by muscle flexing, intimidation, and intervention that solidified the array of anti-Soviet forces it sought to prevent. Even its one longtime non-Communist ally, India—the centerpiece of Soviet Third World policy—was threatening to distance itself from Moscow by enhancing its military and high-tech ties to the United States. East Asia, with its unparalleled economic dynamism, was moving ahead—and leaving Moscow out in the cold.

Gorbachev wanted in. Hints of a shift were evident even before the speech: Vladivostok was foreshadowed by Gorbachev's report to the Twenty-seventh Party Congress and an April 24, 1986, statement (see Appendix C) on the Asia-Pacific region.[3] The watershed speech was a repackaging of ideas that had already surfaced, but it was also a way of submerging areas of continuity in Soviet policy beneath a new style, new attitudes, and a new sense of direction.

Vladivostok did, indeed, reveal a new strategy. First, Gorbachev remolded Moscow's image. As in Europe, Gorbachev mounted a "charm offensive" in Asia, projecting a conciliatory, flexible, and moderate tone, appearing to offer something to everyone. This tactic was reinforced by the frenetic pace of Soviet diplomacy. If the Soviet Union can be legitimized as a valid economic and political actor in the Pacific Basin, Moscow may attain its two main objectives—linking the Soviet economy to the West and linking the development of Siberia and the Soviet Far East to the economy of the region. (Thus the political symbolism of staging the initiative at Vladivostok.) At the same time, by pursuing broader ties with the non-Communist states in the region—emphasizing the economic dimension—Gorbachev hopes to unfreeze the geopolitical status quo and foster a new political environment, more favorable to the Soviet Union and more problematic for the United States.

Gorbachev offered an olive branch to all actual and potential Soviet partners in the region. Where Japan had been denounced for its militaristic behavior, Gorbachev hailed Tokyo as "a power of front-ranking importance," praising its "striking accomplishments in industry, trade education, science, and technology" (accomplishments, it should be added, that Gorbachev hopes to harness to Soviet economic modernization). Where ASEAN had been derided as an anti-Soviet grouping, Gorbachev emphasized that "there is no small amount of things positive in the activities of ASEAN." He declared that Moscow was ready to join with ASEAN in economic cooperation and expanded ties.

The American Angle

Though focusing on the multipolarity of the Pacific Basin, Gorbachev recognizes that the chief rivalry in the region remains between Washington and Moscow: "The U.S. is a great Pacific power. . . . without its participation, it is impossible to resolve the problem of peace and security in the Pacific Ocean." While decrying U.S. "large-scale measures to build up armed forces in the Pacific" and the "militarized triangle of Washington, Tokyo and Seoul,"[4] Gorbachev offered a host of disarmament proposals. In essence, Gorbachev's initiatives seek to turn the liability of Moscow's military presence into an asset. This is perhaps the most misunderstood aspect of his new approach to Asia.

At Vladivostok, and then a year later in an extraordinary interview with *Merdeka,* an Indonesian weekly (see Appendix D), commemorating the first anniversary of Vladivostok, Gorbachev proposed wide-ranging arms control measures. These included: creating nuclear-free zones in the Korean Peninsula and in Southeast Asia; reduced naval activity in the Pacific and limiting naval exercises; a freeze on the deployment of nuclear-capable aircraft; curbs on antisubmarine warfare (ASW) activity; and nuclear-free zones at sea. Gorbachev even said that "if the U.S. gave up military presence, say, in the Philippines, we would not leave this step unanswered,"[5] perhaps by leaving its bases in Vietnam.

As Sino-Soviet rapprochement is a key strategic pillar of Gorbachev's Asia policy, the integration of Siberia and the Soviet Far East into the capitalist economies of the Pacific Basin over the long term is a key economic pillar of that policy. With masterful public relations skill, Gorbachev used the *Merdeka* interview to announce his readiness to destroy Soviet SS-20 missiles in Asia, eliminating the final major obstacle to the Intermediate-range Nuclear Forces Treaty (INF). This concession bestowed an aura of reasonableness on his other proposals. And clearly, in the perception of many nations in the region, Gorbachev's antinuclear initiatives provide the Soviets with a moral equivalence if not one-upmanship versus the United States. Bold-sounding proposals that have little effect on the Soviet military posture allow Gorbachev to project a benign image while making the U.S. posture more vulnerable. By altering regional threat perceptions, Gorbachev's intent is to erode the U.S. alliance network.

On close inspection, there is a cynical and manipulative asymmetry to most of his proposals. Soviet nuclear forces are deployed in Soviet Asia or adjacent waters, particularly the Sea of Okhotsk, where they would be largely unaffected by the new initiatives. Moscow has no nuclear presence in the South Pacific or the Korean Peninsula, where the U.S. presence has been a basic element of deterrence in the region. The proposals allow Gorbachev to de-emphasize the military factor without substantially compromising Soviet deployments, but all would reduce the effectiveness of the United States's primarily sea-based deterrent. While they may signal a genuine Soviet desire to initiate an arms reduction dialogue in Asia, the specific content of Gorbachev's proposals evokes the old axiom "What's mine is mine and what's yours is negotiable."

The China Factor

One of the truly new initiatives, and one of the primary aims, of Vladivostok—and the centerpiece of Gorbachev's Asia policy—is rapprochement with China. Gorbachev offered substantive as well as symbolic overtures to accelerate the hitherto incremental pace of Sino-Soviet detente: the withdrawal of six regiments from Afghanistan; a pledge to withdraw a division of troops from Mongolia; a desire to resolve the Cambodia conflict.

Afghanistan, the Soviet buildup along the Chinese border, and Cambodia comprise the "three obstacles" that China's paramount leader, Deng Xiaoping, has stressed as impediments to full normalization of relations. The Mongolian division was withdrawn (leaving four Soviet divisions there); the Afghan announcement presaged the settlement finally reached last April, and movement toward resolving the Cambodia conflict is proceeding, however slowly.

The one indisputably substantive concession unveiled at Vladivostok was the acceptance of the Chinese position that the Sino-Soviet border lies not along the banks of the Amur and Ussuri Rivers, but in the channel course. This was a rare unilateral Soviet territorial concession that did not go unnoticed in Beijing. Border issues have always been sticky, and the river islands were the scene of bloody armed clashes in 1969. Gorbachev's proposals to jointly develop the river basin, and his implicit invitation to reopen border talks, were well received and helped accelerate Sino-Soviet movement toward detente. Formal resolution of the border issues has been brought within reach; if realized, this could have wideranging ramifications for the geopolitics of the Pacific Rim (see Chapter 4).

Siberia: The Pacific Connection

Thus Gorbachev chose the politically symbolic Siberian venue of Vladivostok to publicly fashion his Asia policy, and spoke of converting the city into an international trading center, because Siberia is a critical component of his Asia policy.

More than half of the Vladivostok speech was devoted to internal matters relating to the Soviet Far East (including western Siberia, Central Asia, and Kazakhstan). Curiously, this portion, much of which focused on the need to apply perestroika to the development of Soviet Asia, is excised from subsequent Soviet reproductions of the address. One important element called for the acceleration of the economic development of Siberia and the Far East by integrating them with the capitalist economies of the Pacific Basin. A striking symbol of this intent was the staging of a trade fair at Vladivostok—previously closed to foreigners because of sensitive military facilities located there—in May 1987. The event was attended by dozens of Japanese business and government officials.[6]

Gorbachev provided details of his intent in a major Asia speech at Krasnoyarsk on September 16, 1988. He revealed a set of market-oriented economic policies for the Soviet Far East that Moscow is considering that would grant Soviet enterprises wide autonomy and create Chinese-style Special Enterprise Zones (SEZs). Under the innovative policies, Soviet enterprises and cooperatives would be allowed to: import consumer goods; begin direct exports and direct ties with foreign firms; enjoy tax holidays on profits and reinvestment; and use hard currency earnings for "social development." The SEZs would permit preferential customs duties, licensing of foreign economic transactions, and reduced taxes. The SEZ concept appears to be a clear effort to lure Japanese and Korean investment.

The catalog of resources east of the Urals is nothing short of spectacular. It accounts for 60 percent of current Soviet oil and gas production, some 80 percent of its fuel reserves (especially coal), and 82 percent of its hydroelectric potential.[7] Moreover, the region contains major (and still largely unexploited) sources of gold, diamonds, nickel, timber, tungsten, tin, boron, lithium, and other hard-currency-earning minerals. It also accounts for half of the Soviet Union's aluminum production.[8]

Given the vast distances, harsh climate, lack of infrastructure, inadequate labor, and resource constraints involved, the development of these resources would be a daunting task under any circumstances. Indeed, without foreign capital and technology, it is difficult to imagine any large-scale accomplishments. Moreover, most of the resources of Siberia west of Lake Baikal, particularly oil and gas, have been developed to service industry in the European USSR. And Gorbachev's emphasis on renovating existing industry in the western sector will further limit efforts to develop eastern Siberia and the Far East for the near term.

Nonetheless, Gorbachev is concerned about the economic stagnation of the region. Even prior to Vladivostok, he stressed that Soviet modernization should "give paramount attention to Siberia and the Far East . . . the development of rich oil-and-gas, coal and other energy resources . . . create additional important prerequisites for more active USSR participation . . . with countries in Asia and in the Pacific."[9]

Some analysts argue that although the current focus of industrial renovation is on the western region, plans to develop Siberia and the Far East are part of Moscow's long-term perestroika agenda.[10] Moreover, Gorbachev's closest economic adviser, Abel Aganbegyan, was the chief economic planner for Siberia for many years and favors a regional approach to development that is unlikely to exclude Siberia. The main indication of Soviet plans for the Far East is likely to be the fate of the Baikal-Amur Mainline Railway (BAM), the centerpiece of the region's infrastructure. The still uncompleted BAM was heralded by Brezhnev as "the project of the century" when it was launched in 1974.[11] Ultimately, it will link Soviet Asia to Pacific ports and stretch to the western portions of the USSR. Although all two thousand miles of rail have been laid, it is barely 50 percent operational. While spending a week in the region—during which he gave the Vladivostok speech—Gorbachev failed to even mention the project. Despite the present de-emphasis, its completion sometime in the 1990s appears to be part of a thirty-year, three-stage plan to develop the region.[12] It is in this long-range context that Gorbachev's approach to Asia is perhaps best viewed.

The Bureaucratic Factor

A critical aspect of the "new look" of Soviet policy toward Asia has been bureaucratic and personnel changes in the Soviet policy apparatus responsible for Asia, which mirror changes at the top levels. In retrospect, it appears that the Vladivostok speech was the result of a major policy review. At about the same time, Foreign Minister Shevardnadze completely reorganized the foreign affairs ministry section dealing with Asia, dividing it into three departments: a Pacific department is now responsible for Japan, Australia, New Zealand, and the Pacific islands; a Southeast Asia department handles ASEAN states; and a third department handles Asian socialist states.[13]

This structural reform was accompanied by a housecleaning of Asia specialists in both the party and foreign ministry. Igor Rogachev, a veteran China hand, replaced the crusty hard-liner Mikhail Kapitsa as deputy foreign minister for the entire Asia-Pacific region. Gorbachev has put another well-regarded Sinologist, Viktor Sharapov, on his personal staff, and appointed Yevgeny Primakov, head of the Institute of International Economics and International Relations (IMEMO), to lead a new National Committee for Asia-Pacific Economic Cooperation. At the ambassadorial level, Gorbachev has put in place a sophisticated team in Tokyo, Manila, and Beijing: Nikolai Solov'yev, a suave, Japanese-speaking diplomat, became ambassador to Japan; Oleg Sokolov, a forty-ish Americanist, is ambassador to the Philippines; and former UN Ambassador Oleg Troyanovsky was dispatched to China.

These sweeping changes have purged the Soviet bureaucracy of the senior officials most responsible for the hard-line orthodox views on China, Japan, and ASEAN, and replaced them with younger, more energetic, and flexible representatives. For example, seventy-six-year-old Central Committee liaison official Oleg Rakhmanin, a conservative skeptic of China's post-Mao reforms, was ousted at the end of 1986, replaced by Vadim Medvedev, a younger technocrat, who quickly rose to a key Politburo post. But like Gorbachev himself, the Asia team has yet to discard much of the political baggage of the Brezhnev era.

Beyond the Brezhnev Legacy

While there is unmistakably a new agenda for Asia and a different conceptual framework, the heavy weight of the Brezhnev legacy is still evident in several areas of continuity with past policy. (There are still some Brezhnev-era holdovers—most notably Ivan Kovalenko, a hard-line Japan specialist in the International Department.) However imaginative Gorbachev may appear in trying to forge a new Pacific order, he also must appear a tough-minded defender of Soviet national interests. In Asia, the infrastructure upon which Soviet policy has been built is Moscow's military posture, which may explain the persistent emphasis on reducing security threats as a prelude to a new framework that would permit the dismantling of some of Moscow's military assets.

One continual theme in Gorbachev's Asia policy, for example, is the call for an Asian collective security conference. Though reminiscent of Brezhnev's 1969 proposal for an Asian version of the Helsinki accords (where Brezhnev's goal was to isolate China), Gorbachev's intention appears to be the isolation of the United States. He first proposed it in a speech at a May 1985 Moscow banquet for Indian leader Rajiv Gandhi and has subsequently raised the idea in every major Asia proclamation, despite the fact that it received only lukewarm support from the Soviet Communist client states and generated even less enthusiasm beyond that.[14]

The general goal of such a forum appears to be to reverse Moscow's strategic disadvantage through diplomacy. An Asian collective security conference would presumably codify many of the measures Gorbachev has proposed (nuclear-free zones, naval limits) that would constrain U.S. military capabilities, erode U.S. alliances, and freeze current borders. But in Asia a Helsinki-type framework is simply inapplicable. Where Helsinki sanctified generally accepted borders, in Asia there is a plethora of unresolved border disputes, armed conflicts, and national rifts (North Korea-South Korea, China-Taiwan). A clue that Gorbachev's motives may be suspect is that his proposals pay precious little attention to the most pressing security threats in East Asia—tensions on the Korean Peninsula, the Cambodia conflict, and the India-Pakistan nuclear rivalry. The idea, then, for an Asian collective security conference appears to be a nonstarter, despite the fact that building support for it is a part of Soviet long-term strategy.

Gorbachev seemed to acknowledge the infeasability of the "Asian Helsinki" idea in his September 16, 1988, Krasnoyarsk speech (see Appendix E). He unveiled a seven-part package of confidence-building measures and collective security initiatives, dropping the grandiose scheme and instead proposing more modest, if still unrealistic, suggestions. These include proposals for six-nation talks on lowering the level of air and naval activity in Northeast Asia and establishing a "negotiating mechanism" to consider Asian security proposals between the United States, Soviet Union, and China as permanent members of the U.N. Security Council.

Another area of continuity in Soviet policy is Gorbachev's emphasis on maintaining Soviet ties to its Communist client states in the region, and its traditional ties to India. Moscow has fortified its security relationship with North Korea, and despite a number of differences, pledged to increase economic support for Vietnam. This parallels the maintenance of Soviet commitments elsewhere in the Third World, such as in Angola and Syria. Despite a recognition that military prowess does not necessarily enhance political influence, Gorbachev must proceed cautiously in disentangling the Soviet Union from past commitments. Thus he emphasizes "national reconciliation" to resolve regional conflicts—a diplomatic method of permitting retreat with honor.

Gorbachev's defections from the Brezhnev agenda, however, are at least as important as the continuities. It is difficult to overstate the importance of the unprecedented Soviet withdrawal from Afghanistan and abandonment of the Najibullah client regime—it does as much to further the credibility of Gorbachev's Asian agenda as the 1979 invasion did to sabotage detente. Similarly, the INF accord, the border concessions to China, progress on Cambodia, and the withdrawal of a division from Mongolia all appear as evidence of a new political intent. However ambiguous the totality of Gorbachev's Asia policy, these moves have begun to transform the political environment in East Asia. But what is the trajectory of Gorbachev's course in Asia, and what are its chances of success?

• 4 •
Sino-Soviet Detente
and the Strategic Triangle

Sino-Soviet relations are the centerpiece of Gorbachev's Asia policy. It is in this area that his initiatives are clearest, the potential dividends are largest, and the consequences are greatest. To a considerable degree, the success of Soviet policy throughout the Pacific Basin depends on Sino-Soviet accommodation.

Rapprochement between the two Communist giants promises to rearrange the geopolitical landscape not only in East Asia but in South Asia as well. In fact, it has potentially significant consequences for the U.S.-USSR-China strategic triangle, a major factor shaping the global balance of power.

Evolution of Sino-Soviet Detente

Almost immediately upon taking power, Gorbachev declared that Soviet ties with China were of central importance. During the funeral of his predecessor, he met with Li Peng (now premier), head of the Chinese delegation, who addressed Gorbachev as "comrade," and for the first time in twenty years, conveyed greetings from China's party chief Hu Yaobang.

But the improvement in Sino-Soviet relations did not happen overnight. Well before Gorbachev's ascension to power in 1985, there had been a sustained, if incremental, warming trend between Moscow and Beijing. The turning point came in 1982 after Brezhnev delivered a speech at Tashkent calling for greater cooperation. Though the speech was tempered by criticism of China's foreign policy alignment, Brezhnev said, "We have not denied and do not deny now, the existence of a socialist system in China."[1] He stressed support for "one China," contrasting it with America's divided loyalties between China and Taiwan.

Brezhnev's remarks acknowledged post-Mao ideological changes as well as the failure of his own intimidating, coercive Soviet diplomacy. Beginning in 1965, Brezhnev had increased Soviet border troops from seventeen divisions to more than forty and deployed an array of theater and strategic weapons against Beijing. It was also during Brezhnev's tenure that vitriolic, polemical attacks against China became routine discourse, with tensions spilling over into armed border clashes in 1969. And it was Brezhnev who went so far as to approach the Nixon administration about a preemptive strike against China.[2]

When modest attempts at accommodation were rebuffed in the late 1970s, the Soviets decried Deng Xiaoping's reforms as "Maoism without Mao." But when the course of U.S.-China relations looked uncertain as a result of the early Reagan administration's support for Taipei, a less abrasive Brezhnev again tried an approach in the Tashkent speech.

At the time, Beijing seemed to be developing a sense of the limits of the U.S.-China quasi-alliance. As late as 1981 China was calling for a U.S.-NATO-Japan "united front against hegemonism," but soon began to talk merely of three "obstacles" to normalized Soviet relations. Chinese leaders began applying the derogatory term "hegemonism" not only to Moscow but to Washington. The shift in Chinese attitudes reflected a perception that the strategic situation was shifting against the Soviets: They were overextended in Afghanistan and in bankrolling Vietnam's occupation of Cambodia. In Europe, they had lost the battle against the deployment of Euromissiles, and they were facing unrest in Poland.

After Tashkent, Moscow and Beijing began twice-yearly contacts at the vice-minister level and increased cultural and economic exchanges. Between Brezhnev's death in November 1982 and the March 1985 installment of Gorbachev, Sino-Soviet relations were hampered by Soviet succession problems, but the contacts continued and a process of dialogue began to be institutionalized. In December 1984, Vice-Premier Ivan Arkhipov (who was in charge of the Soviet aid program to China in the 1950s) returned to Beijing and signed agreements on economic, technological, and scientific cooperation. From a low base of $300 million in 1982, Sino-Soviet trade grew to $2 billion by 1985.

The stage had thus already been set for Gorbachev. After his meeting with Li Peng in March 1985, he immediately called for better Sino-Soviet relations at a party plenum in April. In July, Chinese Vice-Premier Yao Yilin came to Moscow and signed a five-year economic cooperation agreement. The accord pledged to increase bilateral trade to $3.2 billion a year by 1990, and Moscow agreed to refurbish seventeen factories it had built in China in the 1950s and to build seven new ones. The accord also established a joint economic and technical commission at the vice-premier level.

This injected new momentum into Sino-Soviet ties. Following meetings in March 1986 between then-Premier Zhao Ziyang and Soviet Deputy Premier Ivan Arkhipov, and after a visit to Beijing by Soviet economic planning chief Nikolai Talyzin, there has been a growing stream of exchanges of economic managers and technical experts. It is important to note that these improvements pushed Moscow and Beijing a long way down the road to normalization, though they occurred before any substantial Soviet concessions were made on what Deng Xiaoping called the "three obstacles" to normalized relations (Afghanistan, Cambodia, and Soviet deployments along the border). As a result, China has sought to camouflage the political character of the rapprochement.

Vladivostok: Down to the Basics

But with the Vladivostok speech came the prospect of resolving basic differences and paving the way for a far-reaching, stable detente. Aside from heaping praise on China's reforms, Gorbachev addressed the "three obstacles" by announcing a token troop withdrawal from Afghanistan, the withdrawal of a division of troops from Mongolia, and proposed bilateral talks aimed at a "proportionate lowering of the level of land forces."

Beyond these essentially symbolic gestures was a substantial concession: recognition that the border along the Amur and Ussuri Rivers runs not along the Chinese bank, but "along the main shipping channel." This principle would permit the return of the riverine islands—the site of bloody clashes in 1969. That, in turn, could all but eliminate the remaining boundary disputes—except for five hundred square miles of contested mountain range along the Xinjiang/Uzbekistan border.

In addition, Gorbachev proposed building joint water-management projects as well as a railroad to connect China's Xinjiang region with Kazakhstan. The railway, in a strategic border region, has been agreed to by China. It is an indication of the Chinese perception of a reduced Soviet threat and the utility (for nothern China) of economic cooperation with Moscow. Gorbachev's Vladivostok proposals even included the idea of training Chinese cosmonauts.

All of these overtures were presented in the context of Gorbachev's praise for "the objective advanced by the Communist Party of China—to modernize the country and in the future build a socialist society worthy of a great people." The Soviets, he added, "have similar priorities."

China's initial public response was cautious. It is important to note that China has wielded the "three obstacles" as a political club, at times suggesting that progress on any one of them might be sufficient to warrant (or prevent) normalization. In a September 1986 interview with CBS's "60 Minutes," Deng Xiaoping focused on the one obstacle that Gorbachev had glossed over, Cambodia, as the bottom line. "If the Soviet Union can contribute to the withdrawal of Vietnamese troops from Cambodia," Deng said plaintively, he would "go to any place in the Soviet Union to meet Gorbachev."[3]

Nonetheless, the two nations continued their incremental drift toward normalization. Shortly after Deng's comments, a meeting at the United Nations between the Soviet and Chinese foreign ministers resulted in a February 1987 agreement to resume border talks, which had been in abeyance for nine years. This has led to joint aerial photography of eastern portions of the Sino-Soviet border, an important step in both confidence-building and sorting out knotty territorial issues. And there were other signs of creeping normalization. In spring 1987, during a visit to Eastern Europe by China's Premier Zhao, he restored party-to-party relations with the states in the region, thereby holding out the tantalizing prospect that Moscow could be next. In fact, China even sent a delegation to Moscow in November 1987 to celebrate the seventieth anniversary of the Bolshevik Revolution.

Meanwhile, Gorbachev and other senior Soviet officials have continued to push for a Sino-Soviet summit, which Gorbachev considers the sine qua non of rapprochement. In December 1987, Gorbachev took the unusual step of giving an interview to *Liaowang,* a popular Chinese weekly, to campaign for a summit. Moscow and Beijing moved a step closer to a summit after unprecedented week-long meetings in Beijing in August 1988 between senior Soviet officials and their Chinese counterparts that were aimed at eliminating the final obstacle.

Behind Sino-Soviet Detente

What accounts for this seemingly inexorable drift toward normalization? The driving force behind rapprochement is the primacy of economic reform in both countries. Though impossible to quantify, this is a major new factor in Sino-Soviet relations. The reform imperative compels both China and the Soviet Union to foster the least confrontational international environment so that each can devote maximum energy and resources to internal modernization—and so that each can seek foreign capital, technology, and management expertise. An added incentive for

China is the development of its northern provinces, which are fearful of being left behind by the emphasis on development of China's coastal areas.

While Beijing and Moscow approach reform differently—reflecting contrasting levels of economic development and bureaucratic entrenchment—there are striking parallels between their economic agendas and problems. Although China began with rural reform and the Soviets with urban, their market-oriented policies are similar. Both seek to decentralize control of the economy, stimulate private initiative, and harness foreign capital and technology. In addition, the complementarity of their economies, hard currency shortages, and the potential for barter also are facilitating growing Sino-Soviet economic interchange, particularly along their border regions. Both states are increasingly realizing what they have in common: parallel economic goals (Soviet Deputy Foreign Minister Igor Rogachev boasts that "there is already de facto coordination of the Soviet and Chinese five-year plans");[4] Leninist control of the "commanding heights" of the economy; similar Leninist political structures; and similar problems, such as redefining the role of the party in order to retain its dominance and make it more accountable, questions about how much openness to permit, and how to adjust the political system to absorb the changes resulting from economic decentralization.

The Ideology Factor

For much of the past decade, China's economic experimentation has led to qualitative improvements with East European nations. Well before normalizing ties in 1987, Beijing had intensely studied Yugoslav, Hungarian, and Czech "market socialist" reforms. The Soviets now appear to perceive China in a similar manner. According to Sergei Stepanov of Moscow's Institute of Economics of the World Socialist System, China "is the only other socialist country where the economy and task of reform are on a similar scale with ours. . . . That makes China our main foreign reform laboratory."[5]

The dynamics of reform have also generated important ideological changes. Not only have ideological differences between China and the Soviet Union evaporated, but ideology has become an important unifying force. Gorbachev has (at least in theory) replaced the Brezhnev Doctrine with a general notion of "socialist pluralism." This is a product of the crisis of communism, which spurred market-oriented reforms, and reflects a retreat from Marxian universality toward acceptance of a national content to socialist systems.

If, as Gorbachev has said, there is no "model" of socialism and relations are based on absolute independence, then any policy pursued by a ruling Communist party is correctly socialist. This is reflected in the ideological gyrations of both China and the USSR in their quest for socialist rationales to explain essentially capitalist-oriented reforms. Deng's ideology has been based on his pragmatic maxim, "It doesn't matter if a cat is white or black, so long as it catches mice."

After a decade-long search for appropriate ideological auspices, Beijing finally concocted the rather transparent idea that it was at "the first stage of socialism" at the Thirteenth Party Congress in October 1987—a condition that will persist for at least one hundred years. (In 1956 Beijing had declared it was at "an advanced stage of socialism.") This conclusion, explains Soviet analyst Yuri Kornilov in *Sovetskaya Rossiya,* "clarifies many questions affecting the process of building socialism under China's specific conditions and provides theoretical justification for the national economy's strategy of development. . . . Everything which promotes the attainment of this goal is, in the opinion of the Chinese comrades, socialism in action."[6]

Similarly, Gorbachev has reached back to the 1920s, to Lenin's New Economic Program (NEP), to rationalize free-market reforms under the guise of socialism. Gorbachev rehabilitated Nikolai Bukharin, who opposed Stalin's economic plans, to provide a Leninist cast to his reforms. Moreover, Gorbachev's ideologist, Aleksandr Yakovlev, rationalizes Soviet pragmatism with the Orwellian concept of the "socialist owner." In a speech in August 1988, Yakovlev argued that Moscow's market reforms—private leasing of land, family contracts, self-financing factories, and cooperative entrepreneurs—were not excursions into capitalism, but a new form called "socialist ownership."

As abstract as these intellectual gymnastics may appear, they are hardly academic. Without such ideology, both Communist parties would lose any rationale for maintaining their total monopoly on power. Thus the parallel Chinese and Soviet reforms have transformed ideology from a source of conflict to a powerful force for detente. They mutually reinforce the correctness of decidedly unsocialist reforms, legitimizing the respective roles of the ruling Communist parties.

It is not surprising, then, that with increasing frequency, articles in the Soviet press by prominent analysts have begun explaining Chinese reforms and appraising them positively. Among the most conspicuous was a lengthy piece in *Literaturnaya Gazeta* by Fyodor Burlatskiy, a leading intellectual close to Gorbachev, in June 1986; an equally effusive series of articles appeared in *Izvestia* six months later.[7] Similarly, the Chinese press has devoted increasing attention to Gorbachev's reforms, portraying them in a consistently positive light.

Limits of Detente

This newfound ideological lovefest does not, however, eliminate all Sino-Soviet conflicts of interest. The immutable reality is that China and the Soviet Union are neighbors sharing a 4,600-mile border and are major competitors for influence in Asia; a basic and enduring rivalry of neighboring great powers is a permanent factor in Sino-Soviet relations, regardless of its prominence (or lack of it) at any given historical moment. Soviet officials cannot be oblivious to the fact, noted in a recent Pentagon report on long-term strategy, "Discriminate Deterrence," that China may become the world's third-largest economy by the year 2010. China already has a larger nuclear arsenal than Britain and France combined, and it is rapidly modernizing its nuclear triad.[8]

Nor have Chinese leaders forgotten the dangers of dependence learned from their ill-fated 1950s alliance with Moscow. After courting the Nationalist forces of Chiang Kai-shek during World War II, Stalin quickly switched horses after the Communist victory in 1949 in order to conclude a Sino-Soviet alliance that would secure the long border with China. In the decade that followed, the Soviets delivered some $1.35 billion in equipment and military hardware to China and provided some ten thousand advisers and more than $430 million in economic aid.[9] They also returned the Manchurian ports of Dairen and Port Arthur (occupied during the war) in an effort to demonstrate their good faith.

But a series of events reflecting underlying distrust and nationalistic and ideological conflicts of interest soon began to unravel the alliance. The tension became undeniably visible in 1958 when China rejected Soviet requests for radio installations on Chinese territory and did not agree to the establishment of a joint fleet under Soviet domination. Beijing's explicit refusal, Harry Gelman has written, "was one of the major contributing factors in the rapid aggravation of the dispute that led to the abrupt cancellation of all Soviet economic and military aid to China in the summer of 1960 along with the immediate withdrawal of thousands of Soviet advisors."[10] China's distrust mounted at Soviet refusal to help it attain nuclear weapons capability.

That bitter experience suggests that a brutal *realpolitik* underlies the current rapprochement, even though trends point to the likelihood that it will continue. China has carefully calibrated its response to Gorbachev's overtures. By emphasizing Cambodia as the litmus test for normalization, Deng has maximized his leverage. Regardless of Soviet intentions, Chinese support for the odious Khmer Rouge, militarily the most powerful faction, provides Beijing with veto power over any settlement. In the meantime, Beijing has appeared to give Moscow the benefit of the doubt while testing Gorbachev's intentions.

The next phase for enhanced Sino-Soviet relations requires another round of Soviet concessions. Further compromises on border issues could well put a new border treaty within reach and could lead to the conventional arms control process that Gorbachev alluded to at Vladivostok.[11] Under Gorbachev, Moscow has already thinned out divisions along the border.[12] Given that China has reduced its military by 25 percent, it could be argued that an informal, de facto arms control process has already begun. The vast majority of Moscow's troops along the border are at the lowest stage of readiness, and Gorbachev could easily announce a unilateral pullback of five to ten divisions to entice Beijing to a summit (an event likely to occur in spring 1989) and engage China in a full-blown arms control process. Indeed, a number of leading American analysts both in and out of government surveyed by the author suggest that military contacts between Moscow and Beijing may develop over the next five years.

Whither the Triangle?

Where does a scenario of full-blown Sino-Soviet detente leave the United States? Clearly, it increases the leverage of China, the weakest leg of the triad, within the strategic triangle. The growing trend toward multipolarity has in any case led to more equal trilateral relations, altering the nature of the triangle. Within broad parameters, it is no longer a zero-sum game. The nascent U.S.-USSR neo-detente increases U.S. maneuverability, but Sino-Soviet detente diminishes it, though all three sides of the triangle now enjoy wider latitude without affecting the equilibrium.

The key question is, at what point does Sino-Soviet detente become detrimental to U.S. interests? Certainly, a redeployment of Soviet troops along the Chinese border would fall in this category. But otherwise, a decrease in Sino-Soviet tensions is a factor for stability in Asia. It would increase pressure on Vietnam to withdraw from Cambodia, would likely reduce the prospect of North Korean provocation, and in Southwest Asia it might mitigate Indo-Pakistani hostilities. The resolution of the Afghan conflict is likely to stabilize Pakistan.

Regardless of any reduced Chinese perception of a Soviet threat, Beijing's long-term security concerns and its need for Western capital and technology suggest that it will not abandon its insurance policy with the United States. A return to a 1950s-style Communist alliance is highly unlikely. But within those parameters, Sino-Soviet detente diminishes U.S. leverage, narrows the Sino-American convergence of interests, and is a reflection of Beijing's increasingly unconstrained, independent foreign policy. The resolution of the Afghan and Cambodian conflicts will remove two key areas of U.S.-PRC policy coordination, and may be the harbinger of a burgeoning distance between Chinese and American foreign policies. The hard reality is that, short of the outbreak of a global conflict, China's role as an essentially passive strategic counterweight to the Soviet Union yields fewer and fewer benefits to the United States in the realm of day-to-day foreign policy decisions.

China has long been critical of many aspects of U.S. foreign policy (North-South economic issues, the Middle East, southern Africa, Central America). It has strongly opposed Reagan's "Star Wars" programs because development of ballistic missile defenses by the superpowers would neutralize China's nuclear deterrent and could lead to a destabilizing space arms race.[13]

Until recently, most of China's criticism of U.S. policies had little practical consequence: Beijing has been a marginal player in the Third World outside the peripheries of its border regions. But this has begun to change. In the past year, Chinese sales of Silkworm missiles to Iran and CSS-2 nuclear-capable ballistic missiles to Saudi Arabia have placed China in conflict with U.S. interests in Southwest Asia. Beijing's arms sales policies have baffled U.S. officials; selling missiles to Saudi Arabia, for example, threatens both Iran and Israel, nations with whom China has sought to improve relations. But the larger issue raised by such behavior, and by Sino-Soviet rapprochement, is the extent to which U.S. and Chinese interests are diverging and the implications of this divergence for the assumptions governing Sino-American relations (such as liberal high-tech transfer policies, military aid). Chinese territorial claims in the South China Sea may also trigger Sino-American tension as Beijing develops force-projection capabilities.

One area where differing U.S. and Chinese security perceptions have enormous potential consequences is Chinese attitudes toward Japan. In the past, Beijing strongly encouraged Japan to increase its defense capabilities to counter the Soviet military buildup in Northeast Asia, praised the enhancement of U.S.-Japan security ties, and began military-to-military exchanges with Tokyo.[14] This was reflected in a remark by then-Deputy Chief of Staff We Xiuquan in 1980: "Japan is one of the economic powers and it is entitled to become a big power militarily, too. . . ."[15]

More recently, however, China has both publicly and privately begun to express reservations about Japan's efforts to enhance its military capabilities. A recent *Beijing Review* article chided Tokyo's 5.2 percent defense budget increase for 1988 as a "blow to peace." It added, "Japan's continued increases in defense spending have aroused concern and vigilance amongst neighboring Asian countries, the victims of Japanese invasions of the past."[16] A stream of articles in the Chinese press have repeated such views. Just prior to a planned visit in August 1988 by Prime Minister Noboru Takeshita to Beijing, China muted its apprehension about Japanese military prowess. This was in part due to Tokyo's economic diplomacy, as Japan had signaled China that a $6.2 billion economic credit that was offered during the trip.[17] But China's fear of a resurgent Japan remains a long-term factor in Beijing's foreign policy calculus, providing added incentive for rapprochement with Moscow.

China's discomfort over growing Japanese military power reflects a diminished sense of Soviet threat as well as a growing sense that in the future Tokyo may be a major rival in East Asia. And it dovetails with another trend that has appeared with increasing frequency in the Chinese press in particular and the Asian press in general, namely, the perception of American decline. The seemingly intractable U.S. budget and trade deficits, combined with growing calls for allied burden sharing and talk of American retrenchment, raise fears of a U.S. retreat in the Pacific. A recent *People's Daily* commentary said, "The decline of the No. 1 economic power has become the talk of the town in the U.S. Many experts have written on the topic, appealing to the authorities to adopt remedial measures. Otherwise, the U.S. empire will fall like the Roman empire. . . ."[18]

Huan Xiang, an influential foreign policy adviser, has extended the decline-of-the-United States theme to the Soviet Union: "With the weakening of their economic power, the United States and the Soviet Union can no longer go all out to seek hegemonism as they did in the past, and they are finding it harder to maintain their control over their allies." This view is frequently echoed by top Chinese leaders.[19] The superpowers-in-decline thesis reinforces Chinese fears of Japan emerging as the dominant force in East Asia and provides the impetus for a more assertive Chinese posture. For the foreseeable future, if Japan's military role remains defensive and within the framework of the U.S.-Japan security treaty, this problem appears manageable.

But growing Chinese assertiveness is a trend increasingly circumscribing Washington's community of interests with Beijing. Combined with trade disputes and Chinese sensitivity to U.S. criticism over human rights abuses, China's independent posture will render Beijing more susceptible to Soviet overtures. It is part of a new dynamic in the region that requires a rebuilding of consensus about the architecture of security structures in East Asia.

• 5 •

Northeast Asia:
Plus ça change . . .

Northeast Asia is the strategic crossroads where the interests and military assets of the four major global powers in the Pacific—the Soviet Union, the United States, China, and Japan—intersect. It is also the hub of the superpowers' strategic and conventional deployments in East Asia, which gives tensions in the heavily armed region a global as well as regional character. The Sea of Japan, site of intense military activity, and the Korean Peninsula, where tensions between the stagnant, Communist North and the successful, democratized South (in which 42,000 U.S. troops armed with tactical nuclear weapons are deployed), comprise the most dangerous conflict zones in East Asia. The 38th parallel on the Korean Peninsula remains one of the most explosive flashpoints on the globe, where an outbreak of hostilities would likely engulf all four major powers. Japan's emergence as the world's second-largest economy and preeminent financial power and its placement as the cornerstone of U.S. strategy in Asia and the Pacific further highlight the stakes in the area.

The complex regional security patterns and economic realities help explain why Gorbachev has attached a new importance to Northeast Asia. But his actual policies have been characterized more by continuity with past Soviet behavior than with "new Soviet thinking." The legacy of the Brezhnev era—a heavily militarized approach to the region—has proven difficult to overcome. Soviet relations with Japan have made only marginal headway beyond a change in atmospherics. And rather than reducing tensions on the Korean Peninsula, Gorbachev has deepened the Soviet security relationship with North Korea. There has been, however, a surprising and little-noticed shift toward South Korea.

Soviet objectives toward Japan mirror those toward other non-Communist states in the Pacific: cultivation of economic ties and dilution of their security ties to the United States. Linkups with Japan's financial, industrial, and technological power are particularly important long-term goals of Soviet policy. The Soviets see a natural complementarity in the vast energy and other resources of Siberia and the Far East and Japan's dearth of such raw materials. But there has been scant progress toward any new partnership, and prospects are bleak for more than modest improvements.

Historical Factors

History and geography pose formidable obstacles to any major breakthrough. In particular, there is the central dispute between Moscow and Tokyo: Japan's claim to sovereignty over the Northern Territories, the four southernmost islands of the Kurile chain, occupied by the Soviet Union since 1945. Over the past decade, a growing Japanese nationalism alongside a heightened sense of a Soviet threat has led Tokyo to pursue its claim more vigorously. Despite occasional speculation over possible compromise, Moscow has continued to reject Tokyo's claim outright.

Soviet perceptions of the contentious issue are colored by a history of Japanese aggression. In 1904, Japan attacked Port Arthur, and in 1905, it destroyed the Baltic fleet. In 1918, shortly after the Bolshevik Revolution, Tokyo invaded the Soviet Maritime Provinces, occupying northern Sakhalin in 1920. Japan tried to penetrate Soviet defenses in eastern Manchuria in 1938 and along the Manchuria-Mongolia border in 1939. This background helps explain why Stalin demanded southern Sakhalin and the Kurile Islands as the price of Soviet entry into the Pacific war, a price paid by Roosevelt in a secret agreement at Yalta.[1]

The current state of contention was shaped by the 1955-56 negotiations at which Moscow and Tokyo normalized relations. At that time, Moscow offered to return Habomai and Shikotan—the two islands closest to Japan—by defining them as not part of the Kurile chain, and thus not bound by the Yalta accords. A divided Japanese government agonized over the proposal, finally rejecting it and sticking by its claim to all the islands. Moscow and Tokyo agreed to exchange ambassadors but also to shelve the issue for future negotiations over a peace treaty, an event that has yet to occur.

This began for Moscow what Herbert Ellison has described as "a litany of failure" in Soviet policy toward Japan: "failure to conclude a peace treaty; failure to attract Japanese interest in an Asian collective security treaty; failure to block a Sino-Japanese peace treaty . . . ; failure to secure effective Japanese participation in Siberian development. . . ."[2]

Enter Gorbachev

By the time Gorbachev assumed power in 1985, Soviet-Japanese relations had been all but frozen since the late 1970s. Tokyo abandoned an equidistant approach to China and the Soviet Union in 1978, signing a peace treaty with China with an "antihegemony" clause aimed at Moscow. The Soviets subsequently militarized two of the islands, Etorofu and Kunashiri, where they deployed a full division of troops and twenty Mig-23 fighter jets and built up their Pacific fleet to intimidate Japan and contain the burgeoning U.S.-Japanese military partnership. In the aftermath of the 1979 invasion of Afghanistan, Tokyo supported U.S. economic sanctions against Moscow. And the 1983 Soviet shooting down of Korean civilian airliner KAL007 further aggravated the political climate.

Hints of a slight thaw first came in November 1984 when a Soviet Politburo member visited Japan. The following month a joint conference on Soviet-Japanese trade met in Tokyo for the first time in five years. Moves to resume regular diplomatic exchanges—in limbo since 1978—accelerated when then-Prime Minister Yasuhiro Nakasone used the occasion of Konstantin Chernenko's funeral to meet with Gorbachev. This visit led to the January 1986 visit to Tokyo by Soviet Foreign Minister Shevardnadze, the first such trip in a decade.

The Shevardnadze visit appeared to change the atmospherics of Soviet-Japanese relations. Both sides exchanged invitations for a Soviet-Japanese summit, and Moscow agreed to a reciprocal visit by Japanese Foreign Minister Shintaro Abe. In addition, a host of trade, tax, fishing, cultural, scientific, and technical cooperation accords were signed, institutionalizing the basis for broader contacts and imparting a degree of bureaucratic momentum into the bilateral relationship.

But the most politically significant developments concerned the Northern Territories. Moscow agreed to allow Japanese visits to family grave sites not only in the Northern Territories, but also on part of Sakhalin. Japanese hopes of Soviet flexibility were further raised by a phrase in the final communique that Tokyo interpreted as suggesting that the territorial question could be included in discussions relating to a peace treaty—a nuanced shift in the Soviet position, which had been not to acknowledge the issue.[3]

Gorbachev, however, seemed to dash Japanese hopes during Abe's return visit in May 1986. He gave Abe a stern warning against Japanese participation in the U.S. Strategic Defense Initiative (SDI or "Star Wars") research program and then added that Soviet-Japanese relations must be based on "the understanding that no one will be encroaching on the results of the Second World War and the inviolability of the frontiers."[4] This appeared a retreat from hints of Soviet flexibility on the Northern Territories.

Even the Vladivostok speech, while displaying a new respect for Japan in its effusive praise for Japan's importance and its economic accomplishments, contained more of Brezhnev-like arrogance and intransigence than any new framework for more cordial relations. Japan seemed more offended than encouraged by most of Gorbachev's proposals. In particular, Tokyo registered objections to the passage that called for "profound [Soviet-Japanese] cooperation . . . in a calm atmosphere free from the problems of the past." The term "problems of the past" is Soviet diplomatic code language for the Northern Territories dispute.[5]

Gorbachev's call for a collective security conference to be held in Hiroshima ("Why cannot this city . . . become the Helsinki of the Asia-Pacific?" he asked) was doubly offensive to Tokyo. It raised Japanese suspicions that such a conference would be another effort to freeze current borders. And it upset them that the Soviets did not bother to consult with Tokyo before suggesting Hiroshima as the venue.

The bulk of disarmament initiatives and confidence-building measures proposed by Gorbachev at Vladivostok and in the *Merdeka* interview also appeared to Japan as rather transparently self-serving. Innocent-sounding proposals to limit nuclear deployments and antisubmarine warfare (ASW) activity were in fact aimed at neutralizing the U.S.-Japanese forward strategy of "bottling up" Soviet forces in the Far East and Sea of Okhotsk. Without access to the Soya, Tsugaru, and Tsushima straits, Soviet assets would be unusable, and a second-front option in the event of a major conflict would be closed off.

There has been a causal relationship between the Soviet military buildup in Asia and the Pacific and the development of Japan's defense capabilities (increasingly interoperable with U.S. forces), as well as Japan's greatly enhanced strategic and policy coordination with the United States. Soviet deployment of SS-20 missiles east of the Urals in the early 1980s helped push the consensus in Japan toward closer strategic ties to the United States. Tokyo steadily improved its high-tech air defenses and ASW capabilities to fulfill a 1981 commitment to guard the air and sea-lanes out to one thousand miles beyond its territory. Japan's defense plans for the 1990s include further commitments to improve those capabilities plus acquisition of the Aegis air-defense system and AWACs early warning planes from the United States, as well as enhancing its ASW proficiency. Japan's new SSM-1 cruise missile will greatly improve its sea-lane interdiction capabilities.

Japan's movement toward a global strategic partnership with the West was propelled forward by Prime Minister Nakasone, who had strongly opposed the SS-20s (a position adopted by China and ASEAN). At the 1983 Williamsburg summit, Nakasone formalized Japan's global commitment by formally linking Japan's security to that of NATO.

Gorbachev's unsuccessful efforts to block Japanese participation in SDI research reinforced the menacing Soviet image. Undaunted, Tokyo reached agreement in September 1986 with the United States to partake in SDI research. Subsequently, Mitsubishi was awarded an SDI contract and has begun research and development on a defense shield for the western Pacific. Expectations thus raised by the foreign ministerial exchanges during Gorbachev's January 1987 trip to Japan began to fade. The Soviet press increased its ritualistic denunciations of "Japanese militarism," and in his July *Merdeka* interview, Gorbachev spoke of "dark clouds" hovering over Soviet-Japanese relations. The atmosphere was further chilled by the Toshiba scandal (in which a Japanese firm illegally exported technology to the Soviet Union) and a spy scandal resulting in the retaliatory expulsions of Japanese and Soviet diplomats.

Economic Overtures

The Toshiba affair is particularly critical, as it goes to the heart of Soviet objectives—economic cooperation with Japan. It also triggered a visceral reaction in the United States, becoming a tremendous negative symbol in Washington of both Japan's unfair trade practices (contributing to a $58 billion annual trade surplus with the United States) and the perception that the United States is shouldering an unfair portion of the defense burden. Irate congressmen protested by smashing a Toshiba radio on the steps of the Capitol.

As a result of the Toshiba affair, Japan adopted more stringent export controls on technology to Communist states and reinforced a cautious stance in Tokyo's economic dealings with the Soviet Union.

Japan's trade with Moscow has lingered at between $4-$5 billion a year through most of the 1980s. Though Gorbachev's economic diplomacy has produced modest gains in the past three years, current trade is still below the 1982 level of $5.6 billion.[6] This stands in stark contrast to the $120 billion a year in U.S.-Japanese trade. At the last Soviet-Japanese economic meeting in February 1988, Moscow pressed Japan to participate in what it described as a "comprehensive plan for the development of Siberia and the Far East by the year 2000."[7] Japanese firms are participating in two projects in U.S.-led consortiums, (1) a $6 billion petrochemical complex, and (2) a smaller petrochemical project near the Caspian Sea. A smaller-scale version in western Siberia is still in the early planning stages. While some fifty joint ventures are under discussion, only modest Soviet-Japanese joint ventures in coal exploration and natural gas are under way.

Seemingly undeterred, Gorbachev appears to be gearing up for a new round of diplomacy amid signs of a mid-1988 policy review and a new, two-track approach to the Northern Territories issue. At the official level, there is no change in the Soviet position: there is no territorial question. But in an apparent search for a way out of the stalemate, in several discussions with Japanese politicians and academics, some prominent, unofficial hints of a new bargain have been floated.

One sign of movement came when Gorbachev met in early May with the head of the Japanese Socialist party (JSP), Takako Doi, and spent five hours with a top official of Japan's (largely irrelevant) Communist party, Tetsuzo Fuwa. That Gorbachev spent substantial portions of three working days with these two rather marginal political figures itself suggests that some soul-searching is under way in Soviet policy toward Japan. Though the talks appeared to rehash Soviet arms proposals and prospects for a Gorbachev visit to Japan, the Northern Territories question was raised by JSP leader Doi.[8]

Gorbachev again rejected Japanese claims, but reportedly made reference to the 1956 Soviet offer—return of two of the islands, Habomai and Shikotan (not defined as part of the Kurile chain, and thus not bound by the Yalta deal) upon conclusion of a peace treaty.[9] A similar reference was made by Yevgeny Primakov, head of the Institute of World Economics and International Relations (IMEMO) and Gorbachev's point man on Asia, shortly before Shevardnadze's 1986 visit to Tokyo. Since Gorbachev came to power, there have been occasional flurries of speculation that Moscow would return two of the islands in exchange for expanded economic cooperation.

There were further signs of a two-track approach in July 1988 as the Soviets proposed *unofficial* talks with Japan on defense issues and hosted an unusual visit by former Prime Minister Nakasone. According to Admiral Nikolai Amelko, former head of the Soviet Pacific fleet and an adviser to the Foreign Ministry, such talks would begin with scholars from both nations and later include Soviet and Japanese military officials.[10] Japan quickly rejected the idea as a propaganda move.

The Nakasone visit, coordinated with Japan's Foreign Ministry, included a meeting lasting almost three hours with Gorbachev, an unedited talk on Soviet television, and a speech to leading Soviet academics—all of which forcefully emphasized the Northern Territories issue. During his lengthy conversation with Nakasone, Gorbachev referred to a 1973 Soviet offer to return Habomai and Shikotan, but gave only nuanced hints of any reconsideration of the issue. Nakasone quoted Gorbachev as remarking, "We have to think of something, somehow" to resolve the territorial issue.[11] Nakasone blamed the problem on Stalin, who occupied the islands after World War II, and urged Gorbachev to correct Stalin's mistake.

Regardless of whose mistake it was, any qualitative improvement in Soviet-Japanese relations is intimately bound up in the fate of the Northern Territories. Soviet sources have suggested to the author that Moscow might be flexible on the territories issue if it were treated not as a precondition for improving relations, but rather in the context of an overall enhancement of relations. To provide Tokyo an incentive for such a broad improvement in relations, Gorbachev, with his two-track approach, is intensifying the search for a compromise formula that would resolve the territorial issue in such a way that both sides could live with it. Shevardnadze's visit to Tokyo, expected in December 1988, may provide such an opportunity.

Aside from historical claims, there is a strategic factor at play in the islands issue. The Northern Territories form a natural wall insulating the Sea of Okhotsk, where Moscow deploys many of its most advanced nuclear-armed submarines, from U.S. and Japanese ASW activity. Returning them to Japan would increase Soviet vulnerability. One possible scenario would be for Gorbachev to offer a package deal: give back the two islands, and offer to remove Soviet troops and planes from Etorofu and Kunashiri islands—with their final status to be determined in the future. A variation on this formula was offered by a Soviet academician at a Tokyo symposium (cosponsored by the Soviet Academy of Sciences) last July, while Nakasone was in Moscow. G. F. Kunadze proposed that both sides set aside the legal dispute and exercise joint control over the Northern Territories.[12] If Moscow accepted such an arrangement for Etorofu and Kunashiri, while returning the other two to Japan, the scenario would likely generate some interest among the Japanese. Japan could be granted fishing rights around all the islands. This would hint to Tokyo that it was not settling for half a loaf. In exchange, Moscow and Tokyo could declare the area around the islands a demilitarized zone to prevent ASW activity. Japan would also sign a peace treaty and commit itself to large-scale economic involvement with the Soviet Union.

Creative, self-interested Soviet diplomacy along those lines would erode Japanese resistance to a compromise and put pressure on the Takeshita government to respond favorably. But would such a Faustian bargain, with its potential to severely harm U.S.-Japanese relations, be enticing enough to justify the risks? And would the payoff for Gorbachev be sufficient to even warrant such a strategic gamble? The dilemmas posed by such a "land-for-peace" scenario begin to address the real obstacles to Soviet-Japanese rapprochement.

For Japan, the Northern Territories have become far more than just an emotional symbol of irredentism. They are a living reminder of Japanese fears of Moscow and a convenient excuse to ignore Soviet overtures. Even a deal on the territories would be unlikely to result in more than a mild Moscow-Tokyo detente, though it would raise the hackles of many "Japan bashers" on Capitol Hill. But a Japanese accommodation with the Soviets would likely dilute domestic support for Tokyo's military buildup. The centrifugal pull of Japan's enormous economic, financial, and strategic links to the United States gives it little incentive to embark on a drastic economic or security tilt toward Moscow. This will continue to be the case for the foreseeable future (barring a major U.S.-Japanese rift over trade issues that might lead Japan to pursue a Gaullist option). The simple reality is that the Soviets need Japan far more than Japan needs the Soviets.

The resource-dependency argument has little immediate currency, considering global surpluses of oil and gas. Furthermore, as Japan has moved toward more capital- and knowledge-intensive industries, Siberia's natural resources have become less important. And since Japan is under tremendous pressure from most of its major trading partners to increase imports, switching suppliers would complicate the situation further. Another disincentive to closer Soviet ties is the fact that most of the joint ventures envisioned by Moscow are aimed at exporting to third-country markets rather than toward opening new Soviet markets for Japan. To entice Japanese firms, the Soviets are planning Chinese-style special economic zones in the Far East with more liberal investment terms.[13]

Nonetheless, the removal of recent sources of tension—Afghanistan, the SS-20s, Sino-Soviet quarrels—and the onset of a climate of U.S.-Soviet neo-detente portend that Soviet-Japanese relations will evolve into a new phase of detente, if not rapprochement. At the least, a modest acceleration of trade and investment is all but certain to unfold in the near future.

The complicated asymmetry of Soviet and U.S. deployments in Northeast Asia renders regional arms reductions extremely problematic. A START accord would force some reductions in superpower strategic forces in the Pacific. But the increase in provocative military exercises and activities by both sides—witness the Soviet TU-16 reconnaissance flight over Okinawa in December 1987 at which scrambling Japanese fighter jets fired warning shots—provides ample common ground for arriving at some confidence-building measures that would reduce tensions and the level of military activity in the area. Evidence of Japan's persistent fears of the Soviet strategic threat led to its 1988 Defense White Paper (released in August), which depicted an increased Soviet threat; it triggered a loud, negative Soviet reaction.

Gorbachev and Korea

Both the United States and Soviet Union have contributed to the military buildup and force modernization of their respective clients on the Korean Peninsula. As is the case with Japan, there has been little sign of "new thinking" in either the style or substance of Soviet policy toward North Korea. Gorbachev has unfailingly pursued the course taken by his predecessors in reinforcing long-strained relations with Pyongyang. Soviet interests on the Korean Peninsula are primarily strategic: North Korea borders on the Soviet Union's Maritime Province, where a major naval complex is based at Vladivostok.

North Korea has traditionally maintained a unique position in the Communist world by playing China and the Soviet Union off against each other and, in the process, maintaining its autonomy. Politically, it has tended to favor Beijing: North Korea denounced the Soviet invasion of Afghanistan and the Vietnamese invasion of Cambodia. But when in need of military equipment that China was apparently unable to provide, and in search of Soviet endorsement for the first dynastic succession in the Communist world, North Korean Premier Kim Il Sung visited Moscow in May 1984—his first visit in seventeen years.

During Kim's visit Moscow agreed to long-standing Korean requests for upgraded military equipment to modernize its air force—particularly Mig-23 and Su25 Frogfoot. The apparent price for this aid was overflight rights for Soviet military aircraft, permitting Moscow to establish a direct air link between the Soviet Far East and bases in Vietnam and increased intelligence-gathering capabilities. Nonetheless, the relationship continues to be characterized by a lingering mutual distrust—on the Korean side by fears of a Soviet desire to dominate, on the Soviet side by resentment at Korean ingratitude, unpredictable adventurism, and failed economic policies.

Regardless, Gorbachev continued the newfound momentum that Chernenko started. He not only carried out the delivery of the military hardware, but increased other areas of military cooperation. There was the first Soviet naval visit to Korean ports in an exchange of ships, and in October 1986, the first joint military exercise. Gorbachev more recently provided SA-3 and SA-5 surface-to-air missiles and sophisticated Mig-29 fighters.[14] In August 1985, Gorbachev sent Politburo member Geidar Aliyev to Pyongyang, followed in January 1986 by Foreign Minister Shevardnadze The warming trend continued in late 1986 when Kim Il Sung made a still-mysterious visit to Moscow.

In 1987, Kim Il Sung visited Beijing, reflecting Pyongyang's underlying distrust of Moscow. Kim's personal diplomacy appears to have accomplished its aim—grudging acceptance by both Moscow and Beijing of his son, Kim Jong Il, as his successor. Another major goal, however, met with complete failure: both China and the Soviet Union agreed to attend the 1988 Olympics in South Korea after attempts to reach North-South agreement on cohosting the games failed.

The meaning of this new level of Soviet-North Korean security cooperation is unclear. Moscow and Beijing are both wary of Pyongyang's adventurist policies, and both seek to avoid the outbreak of another war on the volatile Korean Peninsula. Such an outbreak would almost certainly instantaneously draw them into a direct conflict with the United States and probably Japan as well. The long-delayed Soviet decision to modernize the North Korean military was probably the product of the bureaucratic imperatives of the relationship as much as any move to augment the strategic alliance with North Korea. The United States was providing South Korea with a host of next-generation equipment including F-16 fighter jets. Pyongyang had vintage 1950s and early 1960s hardware, and the choice for Moscow was either the unrealistic one of abandoning a geostrategically important ally (and leaving a vacuum for China to fill) or providing modern military equipment. The Soviets have accompanied the hardware with pro-North Korean rhetoric (including support for Pyongyang's denial of blowing up flight KAL858 in November 1987, despite detailed evidence provided by South Korea, the United States, and Japan that North Korean agents planted the bomb), but appear to be modulating the amounts of equipment.

The Soviets may feel their security relationship gives them increased leverage with the North in reducing tensions and reaching some accommodation with South Korea (and gives Moscow a larger role in the diplomatic process) or positions them to better influence events after Kim Il Sung passes from the scene. Another element in Soviet behavior may be an effort to assuage North Korean fears of abandonment as Moscow attends the Seoul Olympics and expands its ties to South Korea. In any case, the net effect of Soviet policy is to increase the military capabilities of North Korea, one of the most unpredictable and treacherous regimes in the world.

North Korea has pursued a seemingly schizophrenic approach to dealing with South Korea. While both sides ultimately claim to favor reunification, the South has sought an incremental reconciliation leading to a "two Germanys"-type situation as an intermediate solution. This would entail "cross-recognition," with the West recognizing the North and the Communist world recognizing the South. The North has refused to accept the existence of a South Korean state and has pressed for reunification on its own terms, as well as for the immediate withdrawal of 43,000 U.S. troops stationed in South Korea. These differing objectives have led countless initiatives to fail. They have, however, been factored into new proposals put forth by Pyongyang and Seoul.

A July 1987 North Korean proposal calls for both sides to reduce their respective armed forces to 100,000 within five years and for the withdrawal of U.S. forces from the South. It also seeks a confederation of both regimes under its control.[15] In contrast, a June 1988 South Korean proposal calls for high-level talks to discuss a range of postal, religious, cultural, athletic, academic, journalistic, and other exchanges as confidence-building measures to foster a dialogue on reunification.[16] President Roh Tae Woo also publicly proposed a treaty modeled after that between East and West Germany as a first step toward reunification. A June 11 commentary in the official Pyongyang daily *Nodong Sinmun* denigrated the proposals, again questioning the legitimacy of the Roh government: "Sitting face to face with such South Korean authorities . . . would amount to ignoring the will of the popular masses. The South Korean people do not want talks sponsored by the authorities. . . ."

As the 1988 Summer Olympics approached, the pace of diplomatic maneuvers quickened, with hints of new flexibility by the North after a July 7 initiative by Seoul. Roh Tae Woo broke new ground in a televised speech, when he proposed a wide range of exchanges, including businessmen, academics, and politicians. He offered to begin "trade"— which would be treated as intra-Korean commerce to avoid any connotation that trade would imply a "two Koreas" reality—and offered to help Pyongyang develop ties to the West.

Roh's demarche spurred a July 21 North Korean response in the form of a letter proposing interparliamentary talks and a nonaggression pact as a prelude to the type of contacts Roh suggested. The tone of the letter hinted at accommodation. It referred to Seoul's parliament as the "National Assembly" for the first time, and rather than stressing reunification it spoke of the need for a "relaxation of tension" and a "way of negotiation for detente." A July 30 commentary in the official *Nodong Sinmun* further suggested that Pyongyang might be viewing the opposition-led South Korean parliament as a backdoor way to concede the legitimacy of the South. It explained that since the two respective parliaments "are composed of politicians of all stripes . . . the joint parliamentary meeting will be able to conduct discussions based on democratic principles and embody the will of the sectors of all walks of life." Subsequent official North Korean statements repeated this notion of the diversity of the South Korean parliament changing the political environment.

Nonetheless, this round—the first political contacts in three years— yielded little progress. The unwieldy nature of interparliamentary talks (655 legislators in the North, 299 in the South) led Seoul to propose talks at Panmunjom to pare down the participants to about 20 to 25 on each side. The talks about talks occurred in mid-August, but the two sides failed to reach accord and agreed to reconvene the dialogue after the Seoul Olympics.

The Olympics marked the ultimate political humiliation and loss of face for the North (which rejected Seoul's proposals that it cohost several events). This was underscored by the decision of both China and the Soviet Union—countries that pass as Pyongyang's best friends—to attend the games.

In the past, the North has pursued a two-track policy of military buildup and terrorism on the one hand and efforts at dialogue on the other. In November 1987, North Korean spies planted a bomb on a South Korean (KAL858) airliner, which exploded in midair, killing 115 people.[17] At the same time, senior Pyongyang officials told Selig Harrison, a veteran Korea-watcher, that they were ready to make peace with the South.[18] This follows a pattern of previous events: as China conveyed a proposal for tripartite talks to the United States in 1983, North Korea attempted to assassinate South Korean President Chun Doo Hwan during a visit to Burma. Such contradictory behavior suggests that beneath Pyongyang's monolithic facade there may be factional policy disputes that could result in major shifts after Kim Il Sung's death. But hard evidence of political wrangling is so far virtually nonexistent.

Moscow's Seoul Connection

North Korea's erratic behavior makes it questionable whether Moscow could exert enough pressure on it to achieve a modus vivendi. But in typical Pacific Basin fashion, some remarkable economic developments may be altering the political environment. North Korea, pursuing orthodox Stalinist policies, has fallen hopelessly behind the South economically: Its gross national product is roughly six times smaller than the $130 billion GNP of the South, while its population is only slightly less than half the size. The North's $2.5 billion annual volume of trade is dwarfed by the South's $65 billion.

Meanwhile, South Korea's economic success has begun to attract the North's Communist allies—China, the Soviet Union, and Eastern Europe. Unofficial economic contacts are booming as the new democratic government of Roh Tae Woo has embarked on an economic diplomacy of Northpolitik. China's trade with South Korea approached $2 billion in 1987, and Beijing has been openly soliciting Korean direct investment. China has begun to view South Korea not only as an important source of trade and investment, but also as an economic model to emulate. Seoul has opened trade offices throughout Eastern Europe.[19]

Seoul and Moscow have also begun to increase a range of unofficial contacts, building on a mild thaw that has permitted occasional sports and cultural exchanges since the early 1980s. Most dramatic are reports that Soviet indirect trade with South Korea may have already reached some $500 million a year. The trade is reportedly conducted between the Korean port of Pusan and the Soviet Asian port of Nakhodka, on ships with third-country flags.[20] Another sign that Gorbachev is seeking to diversify economic partners came when a group of leading Korean electronics firms were invited to a Leningrad electronics fair in early 1988.

During the September Olympics, Gorbachev launched official overtures to South Korea. Moscow sent Mikhail Titarenko, director of its Institute of Far Eastern Studies, to speak at an academic seminar in Seoul. Then, in his September 16 Krasnoyarsk speech, Gorbachev for the first time called for "arranging economic ties to South Korea" and for "diverse forms of cooperation." This initiative coincided with a still more remarkable development: the same week, in a coordinated move, Hungary announced it would normalize full relations with South Korea. These developments appear an unprecedented blow to North Korea, which, at the same time these events were unfolding, was celebrating the fortieth anniversary of its founding. Moreover, Moscow began talks with South Korea on opening a trade office in Seoul.

Beyond the economic contacts, Gorbachev is also making other overtures. In February, the Soviet military attache in Tokyo attended a reception at the South Korean embassy. In another conciliatory gesture, he indicated that Korean residents of the Soviet island of Sakhalin may be allowed to emigrate to South Korea. In October, the Soviets invited Korean opposition leader Kim Dae Jung to Moscow, a remarkable political overture.

For Moscow, these developments have wide-ranging implications. In economic terms, South Korea has the potential to be an important partner. South Korean construction firms are among the most competitive in the world and could play a role in developing the Soviet Far East. Korean consumer goods and electronics could also benefit perestroika—if Moscow attains the hard currency to pay for them.

Aside from allowing the Soviets to establish a political presence in a pivotal U.S.-allied state, South Korea's economic diplomacy may provide Moscow with more leverage over North Korea. Seoul's burgeoning ties with Pyongyang's few allies are further isolating an already hermitlike nation. Over time—particularly after the passage of Pyongyang's aging despot Kim Il Sung—pressure will mount for North Korea to shed its outmoded policies and seek economic engagement in the region as well as conciliation with South Korea. The evolving Seoul-Beijing and Seoul-Moscow relationships are characteristic of political and economic trends on the Korean Peninsula, all of which militate against Pyongyang and toward ultimate accommodation on terms favorable to Seoul—barring a desperate military invasion by the North. Soviet and Chinese economic and other contacts with South Korea already provide a basis for de facto cross-recognition. Moscow will be well positioned to play a central role in the conciliation process.

• 6 •

Southeast Asia:
The Good, the Bad, and the Ugly

Gorbachev inherited a militarized, coercive policy toward Southeast Asia and the South Pacific. The policy, which revolved around a strategic alliance with Vietnam, was formulated to project Soviet power and contain China. There was little effort to establish close relations with ASEAN, considered a latter-day version of SEATO (the U.S. regional alliance that collapsed in the 1960s). Gorbachev reoriented this policy to a three-pronged approach, designed to legitimize a new Soviet economic and political role as well as its strategic one. First, Moscow has placed an emphasis on enhancing ties with the non-Communist states of the region. Second, it has sought to erase its negative image and exacerbate neutralist, antinuclear sentiment in order to reduce U.S. strategic access to the region. Third, it has sought to maintain its alliance with Vietnam.[1]

The region comprising the ASEAN states (Brunei, Malaysia, Indonesia, the Philippines, Singapore, Thailand) and the Communist nations of Vietnam, Cambodia, and Laos, plus a number of small island states in the Western Pacific, has traditionally been of secondary interest to Moscow. All are former Western colonies (except Thailand) with a total population of some 380 million (Indonesia, with 175 million, is the world's fifth-largest nation). Once viewed as dominoes that would collapse in the event of a U.S. defeat in Vietnam, the ASEAN states are now among the most promising in the developing world, politically stable, and averaging about 5 percent annual economic growth (except for the Philippines) through the 1980s.

Beyond its strategic alliance with Vietnam (and close ties to Cambodia and Laos), Moscow had played a marginal role in a region polarized by the Sino-Soviet conflict and the Vietnamese occupation of Cambodia.

The ASEAN states, though theoretically nonaligned, tend to be politically moderate and are in fact closely linked to the Western economic and financial system. In the security realm, the Philippines and Thailand maintain bilateral defense pacts with the United States, while Singapore, Malaysia, and Indonesia have cordial arms-supply and training ties with the United States and other Western nations.

The Cambodian conflict, the principal impediment to stability in the region, has reinforced these pro-Western tendencies. Soviet efforts to enhance ASEAN ties and establish new forms of regional participation are superimposed on this conspicuous Brezhnev legacy: Moscow's strategic relationship with Vietnam continues, its economic support has increased, and the Soviet military presence in Cam Ranh Bay and Da Nang has grown stronger since 1985.

The New Diplomacy

The Soviets have devoted considerable time, energy, and creativity to reinventing their image. Moscow has now begun to make concerted overtures to non-Communist states in the region, focusing on economic issues and disarmament proposals, particularly nuclear-free zones. These overtures serve the dual role of diverting attention from the Soviet military profile and fueling the buoyant antinuclear movement. There has been an increasingly frenetic pace of diplomatic contacts and trade and commercial negotiations with the ASEAN states and, curiously, with several obscure South Pacific island nations.

The most important demonstration of Moscow's desire to prove itself part of the region was Foreign Minister Shevardnadze's unprecedented March 1987 tour of Thailand, Indonesia, Australia, and the Indochinese Communist states. The Soviet foreign minister offered little that was new, however, essentially reiterating Gorbachev's Vladivostok proposals. The result was palpable ASEAN disappointment that Shevardnadze brought no new initiative to break the diplomatic logjam over Cambodia.

Nonetheless, the trip signaled a warming trend in Soviet-ASEAN ties and the acceptance of Moscow as a regional power broker. This tendency is particularly evident in Soviet relations with Thailand, the ASEAN state closest to China. Subsequent to Shevardnadze's trip, Thailand's foreign minister visited Moscow, followed by an unprecedented visit by the Thai army chief of staff, Chaovalit Yongchaiyut. Chaovalit discussed not only regional concerns—particularly the level of Vietnamese military incursions across the Thai border—but also the possibility of Thai military cooperation with Moscow.[2] In January 1988, Soviet Deputy Defense Minister Y. F. Ivanofskiy went to Bangkok.

The volume of diplomatic traffic between ASEAN and Moscow has remained remarkably high. In July 1987, Malaysian Prime Minister Mahathir bin Mohamad trekked to Moscow. In May 1988, Thai Prime Minister Prem Tinsulanonda made a similar journey, primarily to help resolve the Cambodia issue. Indonesian Prime Minister Suharto is due in Moscow in late 1988, and Soviet and Indonesian foreign ministers have met three times in the past year.

One largely unspoken factor behind ASEAN receptivity to Moscow is fear of Beijing. (Indonesia and Malaysia are particularly concerned.) This fear will only grow over time as China modernizes. It is based not only on China's size, dominant regional role, and past support for Communist parties, but also on the substantial ethnic Chinese populations in ASEAN states. These groups tend to play disproportionately large economic roles in Indonesia, Malaysia, and Thailand and have active ties with Beijing. There has been frequent domestic tension between ethnic Chinese and native Malays in Malaysia and Indonesia (where Chinese-language publications were banned until recently). This factor also portends an element of long-term Sino-Soviet competition in the region.

For Moscow, there seems a clear intent behind all this activity: it wants to do business with the mid-level developing countries that have the potential of helping the Soviet Union become more competitive through economic interaction. In addition to a steady flow of Soviet trade delegations, Moscow has pushed hard to be included in regional economic forums. Soviet observers have attended the semiofficial Pacific Economic Cooperation Council (PECC), and Moscow has attained observer status in the Asian Development Bank (ADB). Soviet diplomats have also begun pressing for a regular dialogue with ASEAN, as the United States has. This was mentioned by Gorbachev in an unusual message sent to Philippine President Corazon Aquino in December 1987 when she hosted an ASEAN summit.[3] (See Appendix F.)

Certainly, there is far greater economic complementarity between ASEAN and the Soviet Union than there is between Moscow and the West. If perestroika succeeds, Moscow could conceivably pursue a "T-shirts for tractors" strategy: trade Soviet capital goods for the electronics and consumer goods that the more advanced developing states could provide. The pressures of protectionism and competition compel ASEAN to view the Soviets as an attractive potential market.

But so far, the Soviets have not achieved any substantial economic engagement in Southeast Asia. In fact, Soviet-ASEAN trade has been steadily declining from its 1980 level of $1 billion.[4] Total Soviet trade with ASEAN in 1987 amounted to $613 million (compared with $29 billion in ASEAN-Japan trade and $24 billion in ASEAN-U.S. trade). And that trade is heavily tilted in ASEAN's favor, with Moscow importing raw materials (such as rubber and palm oil from Malaysia, with which it had a $144 million trade deficit in 1987). One exception is Singapore, with which Moscow has several joint ventures in shipping repairs, seafood processing, and other service-sector activity, particularly the Moscow Narodny Bank. The bank has also been active in financing East-West trade, with a total exposure of $550 million.

Moscow does not have much to offer ASEAN in the way of economic aid either. Some 90 percent of Soviet aid goes to Communist LDCs—much of it in the form of subsidies, particularly oil.[5] And since world oil surpluses and growing competition are reducing Moscow's two main sources of hard currency—oil and arms sales—Soviet resources are certain to be even more constrained in the near future. Soviet economic initiatives have thus been small-scale ventures just to get a toe in the door—offers to buy Thai rice or a $500,000 order of Philippine sandals.

If Gorbachev does modernize the Soviet economy, medium- and long-term prospects for economic collaboration with ASEAN might improve. But the immediate reality is that Moscow has little to sell and little hard currency with which to buy. In fact, Moscow's economic involvement in the entire Pacific Basin is limited. According to Soviet statistics, total Soviet trade with Asia and the Pacific (including the United States and Canada) totaled 17.3 billion rubles in 1987, 14 percent of total Soviet trade. These figures strongly suggest that for Soviet policy, economics is the handmaiden of politics. It could also be the handmaiden of technology, as economic ties would increase the possibilities for technological leaks to the USSR. This has already become a U.S. concern in the still-embryonic indirect trade between the Soviets and South Korea and Taiwan.[6]

Nuclear Nightmares

One noneconomic Soviet goal seems relatively achievable in the short term: undermining U.S. influence, chiefly through championing of the antinuclear movement in the South Pacific. Moscow has lavished praise on New Zealand's Labour party government for its refusal to allow U.S. nuclear-armed ships to visit its ports. A New Zealand law codifying the ban was passed in 1985, triggering the U.S. decision to exclude the country from ANZUS activities. Less than a year later, Soviet Deputy Foreign Minister Mikhail Kapitsa visited New Zealand—the first such high-level Soviet visit—stumping for the antinuclear cause.

In addition, the Soviets signed the Treaty of Rarotonga, which created a nuclear-free zone in the South Pacific (SPNFZ). The United States opposed the treaty even though Australia carefully crafted its language to exclude a ban on visits by nuclear ships. The Soviets are also strongly encouraging ASEAN efforts to create a nuclear-free zone in Southeast Asia (ZOPFAN). One Soviet objective in this campaign appears to be to create the perception of moral equivalency between the superpowers, not only to supersede negative images associated with Soviet behavior in Indochina and Afghanistan but also to put the United States on the defensive. The impetus for the antinuclear movement, however, comes largely from French nuclear testing in the area—an activity that Washington has supported—not primarily from U.S. activities themselves.

One of Gorbachev's more imaginative demarches was establishing links with two tiny Pacific island states, Kiribati and Vanuatu. Ironically, one of Moscow's chief allies in this venture has been the U.S. tuna boat lobby. The U.S. tuna fishing industry had refused to acknowledge the offshore fishing rights of South Pacific states. In 1985, Moscow offered Kiribati $1 million for fishing rights. After that accord expired, Moscow signed another in January 1987 for $1.5 million with Vanuatu, which included port calls for Soviet ships, an unprecedented development. To counter these moves, the United States agreed to a five-year, $60 million aid package that will benefit a number of South Pacific island states.

Philippines: Testing the Waters

Soviet behavior in the Philippines offers a particularly poignant example of this strategy of denying access to the United States: a New Zealand-type antinuclear strategy—in a country where antipathy toward U.S. bases is a popular cause—could deal a severe blow to the U.S. military posture in Asia. The nuclear issue will undoubtedly shape Manila's position on renewing U.S. base rights to Clark Air Field and Subic Bay Naval Station when they expire in 1991. The new Philippine constitution contains a clause banning nuclear weapons on its soil unless the president deems their presence in the national interest. Legislation now pending in Manila's parliament would toughen the law and remove executive flexibility. Gorbachev suggested in his Vladivostok speech that if the United States removed its bases, "you would not find our response wanting." This vague hint that Moscow might be willing to trade Cam Ranh Bay and Da Nang for Clark and Subic Bay has been repeated in formulalike fashion by Soviet diplomats on several occasions. Gorbachev himself upgraded the idea from a hint to a formal trade-off offer in a Spetember 16, 1988, speech at Krasnoyarsk that focused on Asian issues.

The Philippines, in fact, provides an intriguing litmus test of Soviet intentions in Asia. Gorbachev got off to a clumsy and embarrassing start with the Aquino government. Moscow's major faux pas was underestimating the opposition during the struggle for democracy and denouncing U.S. pressure on Marcos. The Soviet ambassador was the only foreign diplomat to congratulate Marcos on his February 1986 election victory—less than twenty-four hours before the Marcoses were winging their way to exile in Hawaii after a popular uprising in support of Cory Aquino, from whom Marcos tried to steal the election.

Gorbachev quickly replaced the Soviet ambassador to the Philippines and began to cultivate the Aquino government. The new Soviet ambassador, Oleg Sokolov, has on several occasions publicly assured Aquino that "we will never interfere in the internal affairs of the Philippines." Moscow has begun to offer economic aid—a $350 million electrical engineering plant in a joint venture with Finland.[7] The Soviets have also proposed other projects including setting up a ship-repair facility in Cebu, a possible $30 million project.[8] In addition, Moscow has requested permission to open consulates in Cebu and in Davao, in Mindanao (a major locale of Communist New People's Army guerrilla activity), which would likely enhance its intelligence-gathering activities. For its part, the Philippines, through Aquino's enterprising ambassador to the Soviet Union, Alex Melchor, has promoted still other projects, including sending Philippine workers to Siberia.

The Soviets have engaged in a high-profile selling job in the Philippines to create a link between their calls to reduce superpower military competition in the region and Philippine antibases sentiment. On several occasions, Ambassador Sokolov has stressed Soviet opposition to foreign bases while pushing Gorbachev's Asian disarmament proposals. In an unusual, lengthy January 1988 interview with the *Manila Chronicle,* he explained, "We believe that the withdrawal of the bases would be more becoming for the security of the entire region."

During a visit to Manila in late March 1988—just days before Washington and Manila began a review of the base treaty—Soviet Deputy Foreign Minister Rogachev stepped up the campaign. "The sooner these bases are removed," he said bluntly, "the better will be conditions for peace and stability in the Asia-Pacific region."[9] When pressed, Rogachev said that, if asked by Manila, Moscow would "consider" requests to help verify whether the United States had nuclear weapons at Clark and Subic Bay. He called Gorbachev's Asian disarmament proposals a prescription for "drastic reductions" in the military presence of both superpowers.

This is less statesmanship and diplomacy than gamesmanship and psychological warfare. Absent from the discussion are Soviet assets, which are primarily nonnuclear (Cam Ranh Bay) or nonexistent. The disingenuous character of such Soviet propaganda efforts is remarkably similar to the Soviet campaign in Europe in the early 1980s to block the deployment of Pershing-2 missiles. Thus far, there is no sign that Moscow is prepared to put any significant portion of its deployments on Soviet territory on the table, and the Cam Ranh Bay trade-off would not dramatically alter the Soviet military posture.

The bottom line on Soviet intentions in the Philippines, however, is its involvement with the local Communist forces (CPP/NPA). The Philippines has the largest Communist insurgency in Asia, with some 24,000 NPA guerrillas active in 69 of 74 provinces. Moscow's restraint in intervening in support of revolutionary groups in the Third World since Afghanistan may be tested in the Philippines, where the situation offers a rare target of opportunity.

The CPP/NPA has for most of its twenty years been a remarkably insular, if Maoist-oriented, group. It was critical of the Chinese for their close ties to the United States and sharply critical of Moscow for its role in Afghanistan and Cambodia. Until recently, it had minimal contact and only sporadic, marginal support from external sources. But over the past several years, the NPA and its front groups have increased their contacts and shifted their ideological stance. In July 1986, the CPP monthly newspaper *Ang Bayan* declared, "We must expand and intensify our international solidarity work and link it directly with our revolutionary struggle." Former CPP Chairman Rodolfo Salas was more explicit when interviewed in his jail cell. In January 1987, he told *Yomiuri Shimbun,* a leading Japanese daily: "During the past three years, various socialist countries and revolutionary organizations have made proposals for providing us with well-intentioned material aid . . . these countries have included the USSR and Vietnam. . . ."

There is a growing body of circumstantial evidence that Moscow has increasing direct and indirect contacts with the CPP/NPA and with its front groups such as the National Democratic Front (NDF) and the trade union group, the KMU.[10] U.S. officials have been careful to point out that there is no hard evidence of Soviet arms or training for the NPA, and that, in any event, the NPA is an essentially homegrown phenomenon. Privately, U.S. officials have indicated that there are signs that Moscow intermediaries have supplied money to the KMU.[11] In March 1988, Richard Armitage, an assistant secretary of defense, made the first official public assertion of Soviet involvement. In testimony before the

House foreign operations subcommittee, Armitage said that Moscow is among a number of foreign sources (including West European and Australian groups, and Filipinos in the United States) providing money to the CPP. Soviet officials strenuously deny having any relations with the CPP/NPA. Rogachev repeated this assertion while in Manila.

On balance, the evidence suggests that Moscow is testing the waters, keeping its lines open to the CPP/NPA, but has not yet made a decision to support the Philippine insurgents in a significant manner. (This is the consensus view of U.S. officials surveyed by the author.) A decision to do so would not only obliterate Moscow's relations with President Aquino, it would also destroy the receptivity of ASEAN to Gorbachev's overtures. Any intervention—covert or overt—on any scale would shatter what credibility Gorbachev's "new thinking" has attained. It would be a prominent indication of continuity with past Soviet behavior.

The Indochina Conundrum

The most fundamental test of Gorbachev's efforts to fashion a new set of relationships in East Asia is his ability to translate his abstract concept and rhetoric into resolving the key conflict area of the region— Cambodia. In the aftermath of the Afghan accord, the May 1988 Vietnamese decision to withdraw 50,000 of some 120,000 troops from Cambodia reflects new Soviet demarches toward concluding the conflict. But success here is intimately bound up in Sino-Soviet relations and Soviet-Vietnamese ties, both of which are major determinants of the third element, Sino-Vietnamese rivalry.

Soviet-Vietnamese relations have always been a complex marriage of convenience.[12] Their current intimacy has been driven primarily by the "China factor." Until 1978, Hanoi had performed a deft political juggling act, balancing Moscow and Beijing. Sino-Vietnamese tensions, reflected in Beijing's support for a belligerent Khmer Rouge regime (whose border attacks precipitated Hanoi's invasion) and Vietnam's treatment of overseas Chinese, drew Hanoi into its Friendship Treaty with Moscow and membership in the Council for Mutual Economic Assistance (COMECON) in 1978. Moscow, seeking to contain China, seemed to almost reflexively step into the geopolitical vacuum created by the American retreat from Indochina.

The costs and benefits to both sides hint at the limits of the Soviet-Vietnamese convergence of interests. For Hanoi, its alliance with Moscow has provided an insurance policy against China that has permitted it to overthrow a pro-Chinese regime in Cambodia and to pursue a policy of domination over Indochina. Soviet military and economic aid has been critical to Vietnam. During its 1981-85 five-year plan, Soviet aid averaged about $1 billion a year, and the 1985-90 commitment is at least twice that.[13]

The price of Soviet friendship has been steep, however. Hanoi has become dependent on Moscow and isolated from ASEAN, the United States, and Japan. Two-thirds of Vietnam's imports come from the Soviet bloc, with which it has incurred a $7.7 billion foreign debt.[14] Vietnam's isolation has deprived it of Western capital and technology that Hanoi's leaders increasingly view as necessary for modernizing its backward economy.

Beyond economic dependency, Vietnam's provision of military basing rights to the Soviets is another embarrassing compromise of its hard-fought independence. Both Moscow and Hanoi have gone to great lengths to deny that Cam Ranh and Da Nang are actual bases. This denial is the source of many Talmudic debates, but for all practical purposes, they are bases. There is a growing, full-time Soviet military presence at these facilities, including twenty to twenty-five ships, sixteen TU-16 Badger attack bombers, Mig-23 Floggers, and Bear D reconnaissance planes.

For the Soviets, the alliance is a symbol of their global reach. Its military presence in Vietnam enhances Moscow's capabilities in the Pacific and, more importantly, facilitates the projection of Soviet military force into the Indian Ocean from warm-water ports 2,200 miles from Vladivostok. But the military facilities also limit Moscow's leverage on Hanoi in a manner similar to the way Clark and Subic Bay limited U.S. pressure on Marcos. And the drain of scarce Soviet resources is considerable. Politically, Soviet backing for Vietnam has been counterproductive in many respects. It has been the chief barrier to improved relations with China and ASEAN.

Signs of Soviet-Vietnamese discord have increased in direct proportion to improved Sino-Soviet relations. For Vietnam, concern has mounted over what price Moscow is willing to pay for rapprochement with China. This clearly illustrates differing political calculations: Soviet global considerations *versus* Vietnam's regional concerns. The difference was starkly evident in Moscow's response to the March 1988 Sino-Vietnamese armed clashes over the disputed Spratly Islands. Vietnam lost two ships and some seventy soldiers in that display of Chinese assertiveness. Equally disturbing to Hanoi was Moscow's tepid response: it was silent for two weeks before official Soviet comments urged both sides to negotiate a solution.

Disputes over the quality and quantity of Soviet aid—and Vietnam's use of it—have been evident for some time (Gorbachev himself openly questioned Hanoi's use of Soviet aid as a visiting Politburo member in 1982) but have grown more bitter as the Vietnamese economy plunged deeper into crisis. Attending the December 1986 Vietnamese party congress, Politburo member Yegor Ligachev raised the issue. During his 1987 trip to Southeast Asia, Shevardnadze called for both better use of aid and a speedy resolution of the Cambodia conflict, fueling speculation that Moscow might be linking the two issues.

Despite Hanoi's fears, the Soviets have repeatedly stated publicly that Sino-Soviet normalization will not take place at Vietnam's expense. Nonetheless, the Soviets have been increasingly willing to discuss Cambodia with all concerned parties, including the Chinese.[15] The issue was a focal point of Sino-Soviet talks in May 1987. Cambodia was also the preoccupation of the visit to Moscow by Thai Prime Minister Prem in mid-May 1988, shortly before the Vietnamese announcement of its troop withdrawal. The Thai daily, *The Nation,* commented on May 27, "The Soviets, more than anyone else, deserve credit for ending Hanoi's intransigence over its occupation of Kampuchea."

Soviet efforts to assume a key role in brokering a Cambodia settlement reached new heights in August 1988, when Soviet Deputy Foreign Minister Igor Rogachev sat down with his Chinese counterpart for an unprecedented five-day meeting in Beijing devoted solely to Cambodia. The talks, a likely precursor to a Sino-Soviet summit, failed to resolve all their differences. But after more than forty hours of intensive discussions, the talks imparted momentum to the peace process and may have laid the political groundwork for a settlement.

Cambodia: Peace at Hand?

The recent flurry of diplomatic activity—and Vietnam's new flexibility—is in part the result of Soviet pressure on Hanoi and Gorbachev's more activist role, which has evolved since early 1987. Nuanced differences between the Soviets and Vietnamese were discernible during the May 1987 visit to Moscow of Vietnamese Premier Nguyen Van Linh. Gorbachev gave a speech calling for a "political solution" and introduced a new formulation of resolving the conflict "on the basis of the unification of all patriotic forces." Gorbachev's formula hinted at a major concession—a genuine multiparty coalition government. The Hanoi-backed Phnom Penh regime supported a more restrained "national reconciliation" policy that allowed deserters from the opposition to participate in the government.[16] (Moscow has sought to develop direct ties with both Cambodia and Laos since 1978, though it has stopped short of undermining Vietnamese hegemony over both governments.)[17]

After a July 1987 meeting between Gorbachev and Heng Samrin, the Vietnamese-backed Cambodian leader, the Phnom Penh regime altered its characterizations of Prince Norodom Sihanouk, who is increasingly viewed by all sides as the key to any settlement.[18] In October 1987, Phnom Penh issued a five-point peace plan that incorporated Gorbachev's broader definition of national reconciliation, a position Hanoi publicly supported. Later that month Cambodian Prime Minister Hun Sen went to Moscow for consultation. Shortly thereafter, he invited Sihanouk to the first of two unprecedented meetings in France. In December 1987, the Soviets began pressing the Phnom Penh regime to begin direct talks with the Khmer Rouge.[19]

But the Afghan accord gave new impetus to Soviet efforts to broker a settlement. Beginning with Gorbachev's statement in February 1988 that set the May 15 date for the Soviet pullout, he has escalated his rhetoric, emphasizing that the Afghan accord "will have the most profound impact on other regional conflicts," specifically Cambodia.[20] On a tour through Southeast Asia, Soviet Deputy Foreign Minister Rogachev repeated in several ASEAN capitals that Afghanistan provides a "good example" for resolving Cambodia. On May 25, ten days after Soviet troops began withdrawing from Afghanistan and four days before the Moscow summit, Hanoi announced it would withdraw fifty thousand troops by the end of the year.

Since 1986, Vietnam has said it would withdraw its forces from Cambodia by 1990. But a confluence of factors—Soviet pressure, stalemate on the battlefield, and perhaps most importantly, the imperatives of domestic reform (of a basket-case economy)—have led Hanoi to accelerate the search for a settlement. Ultimately, two elements are vital to any viable solution: first, Vietnam's willingness to accept a "Finlandized" Cambodia and abandon its Indochina federation, and second, China's willingness to abandon the dreaded Khmer Rouge, which has done the overwhelming majority of the fighting in a tentative coalition with Sihanouk and Son Sann, the leaders of two anti-Communist groups.

The first major collective effort to come to grips with these issues occurred in late July 1988 at a special convocation in Indonesia, dubbed the "Jakarta Informal Meeting." The product of some two years of Indonesian diplomacy, the gathering included ASEAN, Vietnam, and all four Cambodian factions. Its most visible achievements appeared to be a public airing of the positions of all parties involved, a more lucid sense of where the problems lie, and vague agreement to consider another meeting. But its mere occurrence was a step toward devising a framework for a settlement and provided new impetus to the peace process. It was followed by the Sino-Soviet meeting on Cambodia, which moved the two prime sponsors of the war toward accord, and a third Sihanouk-Hun Sen meeting in November 1988.

The broad outlines of a settlement are now visible: a phased withdrawal of Vietnamese troops in tandem with the cessation of all outside aid; a UN peacekeeping force for an extended period of time; the establishment of a neutral coalition government; and internationally monitored elections. There are, however, many gray areas, and the devil, as always, is in the details. What should be the size, mandate, and composition of a UN force, and who will finance it? How to structure a viable coalition regime? How to merge the four armies into a new national entity? And how to prevent the Khmer Rouge, the largest, best-armed, and most effective army, from sabotaging any accord and returning to power by force? These critical questions remain, but the momentum is clearly building toward a Vietnamese withdrawal and a transition to a new Cambodian regime centered on Prince Sihanouk, the only political figure with unquestioned national stature and wide popularity.

A resolution of the Cambodian conflict would alter the geopolitical landscape of Southeast Asia. It would end Vietnam's isolation and open the prospect of its large-scale economic involvement with the West, Japan, ASEAN, and the East Asian NICs. Over the long term, it would lead to a diminution of Soviet influence in Vietnam. But it may also pose difficult policy choices for the United States. A normalization of relations with Vietnam will undoubtedly follow a settlement. Less certain is the level of U.S. involvement in encouraging Vietnam's political and economic reforms. (*The Wall Street Journal* has described the prospect of these changes as "another revolution.") The U.S. response will have political ramifications beyond bilateral relations.

There may also be a strategic choice facing U.S. policymakers. Vietnam's integration into the region will dilute Chinese influence in Southeast Asia. While Beijing may be prepared to make a short-term accommodation with Hanoi, their two-thousand-year-old rivalry will not disappear. It is not at all certain that a more independent Vietnam, interwoven into the political fabric of Southeast Asia, is perceived by Beijing to be in its interests. It is, however, in the ASEAN interest to see a Vietnam gravitating toward the West emerge as a counterweight to Chinese influence in Southeast Asia. China's emphasis on reducing tensions to permit it to focus on its domestic reforms may lead to an acceptance of such a new geopolitical reality. But over time, the United States may be forced to choose between appeasing China or pursuing a course in Southeast Asia that is in conflict with Beijing's national objectives. An independent Vietnam that is integrated into the region is, however, clearly in the interest of both the United States and ASEAN if it means weakened Moscow-Hanoi ties and the abandonment of Hanoi's efforts to create an "Indochina federation."

Moscow's response to the new realities unfolding in Southeast Asia is uncertain. Its military presence in Vietnam is not part of any Cambodia package and is unlikely to be affected in the near future. A settlement will enhance its status in the region and hasten a Sino-Soviet summit. The glow of a Cambodia settlement lends credence to Moscow's new image and legitimacy to its expanded regional participation. It also obscures the elements of continuity with the past—military deployments, contacts with the CPP/NPA in the Philippines, and its diplomatic efforts to decouple the United States from its allies.

• 7 •

New Sources of Soviet Conduct?

As we have seen, Gorbachev has a programmatic new agenda for Soviet foreign policy in Asia. The change in Soviet strategy, tactics, and style in the two years since the Vladivostok speech has imbued its policy in the Asia/Pacific region with a hitherto missing vitality. Nonetheless— as is the case with the bulk of Gorbachev's foreign and domestic policies—its fragmentary implementation is still characterized by a tentativeness that serves as a source for lingering doubts about Soviet objectives.

Gorbachev's agenda is superimposed on Brezhnev's military-dominated legacy: Soviet troops on the Chinese border; a Soviet division and fleet of Mig-23s in the Japanese-claimed Northern Territories; an overseas military base at Cam Ranh Bay. Whatever credibility Gorbachev has attained for his Asia policy is based on the promise of change, as demonstrated by initial displays of good faith (such as Afghanistan, the INF accord, a potential Cambodia settlement). And while it may be unreasonable to expect Moscow to instantly dismantle what have been the pillars of its policy, it is equally irrational to disregard the residue of threatening capabilities on the basis of putative intentions.

Nothing epitomized the foreign policy of the Brezhnev era more than the Soviet invasion of Afghanistan. That event marked the apogee of a period of expansion and strategic buildup. Never before had Moscow applied the direct use of Soviet troops on a large scale in the Third World. The Afghan invasion was the Brezhnev Doctrine writ large, an event that in some ways changed the world. It drove the final nail in the coffin of detente, creating widespread apprehension about Soviet intentions.

For Gorbachev, therefore, Afghanistan was the acid test of a new foreign policy, the *sine qua non* for repudiating the Brezhnev legacy. The retreat from Afghanistan—the first for the Red Army since 1955 when it withdrew from and left behind a neutral Austria—opens a new chapter in Soviet foreign policy. It is the first *fait accompli* of a still-ambiguous Asia policy, hinting that a new logic may be governing Soviet behavior. A close look at the evolution of the Afghanistan gambit is a good starting point for assessing to what extent that policy reflects new sources of Soviet conduct and, hence, new possibilities for superpower relations.

Not My War: Search for an Exit

Gorbachev can rightly plead "not guilty" for the colossal miscalculation that was Afghanistan: he was a nonvoting member of the Politburo when the still-controversial decision to send in forces was made, apparently by only a handful of senior Politburo members.[1] After six years of brutal conflict, Moscow had little to show for the effort: a standoff on the battlefield and a client regime in Kabul with little credibility. According to Gorbachev, a policy reassessment began within weeks of his ascendancy in April 1985: "The Politburo conducted a hard and impartial analysis of the position [in Afghanistan] and started even at that time to seek a way out of the situation."[2]

Nonetheless, Gorbachev's initial response was to prosecute the war more efficaciously. While he may have had one eye on the negotiating table, in July 1985, he placed one of his most celebrated military officers, General Mikhail Zaitsev, in direct command of the war effort. Zaitsev honed new tactics using the vaunted Spetznaz, Soviet elite units, and Hind-24 counterinsurgency helicopters.

But even at that point, according to UN negotiator Diego Cordovez, who had been pursuing a negotiated solution for three years, "things began to change." Cordovez said that Gorbachev "came up with a number of ideas on how the negotiations should move forward."[3] One breakthrough did occur: in December 1985, U.S. officials, dubious that Moscow would actually pull out, agreed to serve as coguarantor of a settlement along with the Soviet Union.

During Gorbachev's speech to the Twenty-seventh Party Congress in February 1986, he called Afghanistan "a bleeding wound" and said that agreement had been reached with Kabul for "a phased withdrawal" pending political settlement. The Soviet Union, he added, wanted to bring its troops home "in the nearest future." Shortly after Gorbachev's speech, the Afghan regime conveyed to Cordovez its first timetable for troop withdrawal—a preposterously long forty-eight months.

Gorbachev's next move, in May 1986, was the removal of Babrak Karmal, the Afghan leader whom Moscow had installed as president when it invaded in 1979. He was replaced by Najibullah, the stocky, bluff head of the Khad, the Afghan KGB. In retrospect, the deposing of Karmal was indicative of the fundamental problem that eventually led Moscow to write off Afghanistan: the utter inability of the People's Democratic Party of Afghanistan (PDPA), the Afghan Communist party, to establish a modicum of credibility. However effective the Soviet military might be, without some political force that could provide a semblance of legitimate government, Moscow's efforts were destined to fail.

Najibullah was given a mandate from Moscow to pursue a national reconciliation program. At Vladivostok, Gorbachev explained that meant "widening the social base of the April national-democratic revolution, including the creation of a government with the participation in it of those political forces that found themselves beyond the country's boundaries." This was clearly an attempt to reach those rebels and refugees based in Pakistan whom Moscow had previously denounced as "bandits."

In what now appears a symbolic signal of Soviet intent, Gorbachev had also announced a token withdrawal of six regiments, which he said reflected Moscow's "striving to speed up a political settlement." Largely unnoticed in his message on Afghanistan was the significance of his characterization of the government as national-democratic. This denied Najibullah and the PDPA the standard sobriquet "socialist-oriented" applied to aspiring Marxist client states. In Soviet Marxist jargon, as a senior diplomat told me, "this has an important meaning." It meant that ideologically the PDPA had been demoted by Moscow—and was therefore expendable.

Ideology aside, the political maneuvering that followed was remarkably reminiscent of the wrangling that occurred between the Nixon administration and the Vietnamese client regime of Nguyen Van Thieu in the early 1970s during the Paris peace talks. As the Paris accords provided a "decent interval" for the United States to withdraw (in the end throwing Saigon to the wolves), Gorbachev's moves appeared to Najibullah as a policy that held a similar fate for him.

In the latter half of 1986, Soviet efforts to achieve a graceful exit were given a new sense of urgency. The Reagan administration, which had steadily increased covert aid to the Afghan rebels to $630 million a year, upped the ante. Washington began delivering Stinger anti-air missiles to the Mujahideen rebels, quickly changing the nature of the war. The Stingers deprived Moscow of control of the air—the Soviets were at times losing a plane a day.

In December 1986, Moscow sent a high-level delegation to Kabul, then summoned Najibullah and the entire Afghan cabinet to Moscow later that month. Gorbachev reportedly informed them that time was running out. When Najibullah returned to Kabul, he was surprised by an extraordinary visit from Shevardnadze and the CPSU International Department chief, Anatoly Dobrynin. At that point Najibullah began a frantic effort to come to terms with the Mujahideen rebels. He unveiled a "plan of national reconciliation," offering amnesty to rebels and refugees in Pakistan and Iran, a coalition government, and a new constitution accepting Islam as the national religion. Najibullah also announced a six-month unilateral ceasefire.

At the eighth round of UN talks in Geneva in February 1987, the Soviets reduced their proposed timetable for withdrawal to eighteen months, moving closer to the seven to eight months sought by Pakistan. In his July *Merdeka* interview, Gorbachev said, "In principle, the question of the withdrawal of Soviet troops from Afghanistan has already been decided." By November, Moscow had reduced the timetable to twelve months.

At the Reagan-Gorbachev summit, working-level groups made largely unnoticed progress in ironing out some of the final sticking points regarding the modalities of withdrawal. At a postsummit press conference, Gorbachev hinted that Najibullah's fate was no more than a secondary consideration: "We are not seeking any outcome under which there has to be a pro-Soviet regime in Afghanistan. But the American side must clearly say that it is not seeking to install a pro-American regime."[4]

The penultimate move that cleared the way for a settlement was a dramatic statement by Gorbachev in February 1988, when he named May 15 as the day Soviet troops would begin withdrawing. He pledged the process would be completed within ten months. He made a point of separating the withdrawal from the political future of Afghanistan. "This," he emphasized, "is a purely internal Afghan issue. It can only be resolved by the Afghans themselves . . . it is none of our business, or yours, for that matter."[5] Gorbachev seemed to be washing his hands of Afghanistan once and for all. The peace accords were finally signed on April 14.

Why an Afghan Retreat?

However elegantly Gorbachev packages the withdrawal (a magnanimous act for world peace), it remains a stinging defeat. The Soviet withdrawal has inescapable implications of far larger proportions than merely losing a friendly client. It reflects a marked shift in the prospects for socialism in the less developed world and the global "correlation of forces" on which Soviet calculations have been based. As the United States discovered in Vietnam, the ability of even a superpower to work its will in inhospitable Third World environments is circumscribed. And the cost can be enormous: for Moscow, some twelve thousand dead soldiers and perhaps $10 billion or more over the nine-year occupation.

What is truly remarkable about Gorbachev's capitulation is the fact that of all Moscow's far-flung adventures, Afghanistan was the one with the most legitimate security considerations. Unlike Ethiopia or Angola, Afghanistan shares a lengthy twelve-hundred-mile border with the Soviet Union: Strategically, it is to Moscow as Mexico is to the United States. Historically, Afghanistan has been a buffer against great-power encroachment going back to the nineteenth century. Nonetheless, rather than escalate their 115,000-troop commitment (as the United States did with some 500,000 troops in Vietnam) the Soviets chose to leave, accepting an Afghanistan that almost certainly will be politically hostile.

In an unusual confessional article, Graham Fuller, a senior CIA official who retired in 1987, wrote, "I personally felt that Afghanistan was perhaps the last third-world country from which I could ever imagine a Soviet withdrawal."[6] U.S. strategic analysts routinely argued that the Afghan invasion was part of an inexorable Soviet march toward the warm-water ports of the Persian Gulf. In the spring 1988 issue of *Foreign Affairs,* former national security adviser Zbigniew Brzezinski described the Afghan invasion as a "Soviet effort to gain a geopolitical presence in the Gulf." Similarly, writing in 1986, former CIA Soviet specialist Harry Gelman argued that Gorbachev "is unlikely to find it politically possible to get out of Afghanistan on any terms that do not perpetuate Soviet hegemony."[7]

Few U.S. analysts seriously considered the prospect of Soviet withdrawal until Gorbachev's February statement. The conventional wisdom had been that Afghanistan was but another of the Brezhnev Doctrine's irreversible facts. From George Kennan's original "Mr. X" article in 1947 (formulating the containment doctrine) to the present, leading Soviet specialists have argued that expansionism is a vital component of the Soviet system. Former White House Soviet adviser Richard Pipes has written, "The best way to demonstrate the need for a powerful Communist state and military establishment is constantly to expand the Soviet realm." Under Brezhnev, expansionism was one of the sources of Soviet conduct, serving to legitimize his rule and reinforce Soviet ideology.

But one of Gorbachev's departures from previous Soviet rulers is to openly admit (at least the obvious) failures of the Soviet system. The success of socialism is thus defined as remedying these shortcomings and modernizing the Soviet economic and political system, not by the number of Third World states declaring themselves Marxist-Leninist and establishing client relationships with Moscow. The primacy of reform supersedes all other objectives and is disconnected from the spread of socialism. The ideological raison d'etre of Soviet expansionism is absent from this formulation, from which flows a foreign policy of retrenchment.

Nonetheless, Moscow remains a military superpower. Gorbachev must appear a tough-minded defender of Soviet commitments, even as he seeks to shed them. While acting out of a fundamental weakness, he cannot appear weak. In the case of Afghanistan, Gorbachev has so far managed to make a virtue out of necessity by orchestrating an orderly negotiating process that avoided the appearance of defeat and instead blamed Afghan incompetence. The logic was revealed in an extraordinary article in the Soviet weekly *Literaturnaya Gazeta*. Veteran military writer Aleksander Prokhanov explained:

> When we sent in the troops we assumed that their presence would counterbalance the mighty pressure from abroad and the internal civil strife would eventually die down. . . . The PDPA, defining the path of state development, would be able to create an effective structure covering the whole country . . . stability would prevail. It did not happen. The PDPA did not become a force acknowledged by all the people."[8]

Clearly, if such criteria were applied to other Soviet Marxist clients such as Ethiopia, South Yemen, or Angola, Moscow would be left with little justification for its behavior. Skeptics may argue that Afghanistan represents the exception—a product of costly military defeat that left Moscow with little choice—not the new rule. While the implications vary from one ally to another, Afghanistan can hardly send a reassuring signal to any of them. Indeed, Moscow is actively pursuing solutions to regional conflicts in southern Africa and Indochina on a similar model of "national reconciliation." Reflecting a now-common Soviet view, V. I. Dashichev, a prominent Soviet academician, explained the mistakes of the Brezhnev era: "We attempted to expand the sphere of socialism's influence to various developing countries which, I believe, were totally unprepared to adopt socialism."[9]

The notion that factors such as ethnicity, religion, traditionalism, and nationalism create conditions unlikely to produce socialism in developing nations has begun to appear with increasing frequency in the writings of Soviet analysts.[10] "Afghan events," wrote Graham Fuller, "require that we recognize that Moscow may now be starting to operate from a different set of political imperatives."[11] The sense of optimism, of the historical inevitability of a shifting "correlation of forces" in its favor, is noticeably absent from Gorbachev's foreign policy.

New Sources of Soviet Conduct

Indeed, it is instructive to hark back to George Kennan's "X" article in *Foreign Affairs,* the basis of containment policy for the past four decades, to see how, for the first time, the nature of Soviet power appears to be changing. Among the fundamental concepts guiding Kremlin behavior, Kennan explained, was a belief in "the innate antagonism between capitalism and socialism." This leads Moscow to pursue policies of "a cautious, persistent pressure toward the disruption and weakening of all rival influence and rival power."[12]

Another basic concept of Soviet power cited by Kennan is "the infallibility of the Kremlin. . . . On the principle of infallibility rests the iron discipline of the Communist Party."[13] As the sole repository of wisdom, Kennan explained, the party can create and change truth as it sees fit. "It may vary from week to week, month to month." Truth, Kennan explained, "can be changed at will by the Kremlin, but by no other power."[14] Viewed in light of current political realities in the Soviet Union, it is difficult to envision Moscow reverting to the monolithic, stifling nature of pre-Gorbachev power. But the official interpretation of events—as per Afghanistan—is still subject to the needs of the state more than to historical accuracy. Nonetheless, whatever twists and turns Gorbachev's reforms might take, it is difficult to see how the political genie he has unleashed could be put back into the bottle.

Kennan anticipated that the self-delusion and arbitrariness of the Soviet system "bears within the seeds of its own decay." But given the stultifying nature of the Soviet political structure, few would have anticipated a politician with a vision of radical reform reaching the top rung of power and launching a campaign to save the system from itself. As Franklin Roosevelt sought to reform the capitalist system through state intervention in order to save it, Gorbachev has begun to introduce market-oriented policies and political accountability to salvage socialism. No longer must Moscow emphasize the "menace of capitalism abroad," as Kennan explained, "to justify the retention of the dictatorship."

Certainly, both glasnost and perestroika are still in their early stages, with the outcome of Gorbachev's domestic reforms very much an open question. But events in the Soviet Union—from monuments built to honor the victims of Stalin's crimes to dozens of political clubs, and even a "national front" in Estonia—almost daily reveal a very different type of Soviet power unfolding under Gorbachev. Even three years ago, who could have imagined the spectacle of the June 1988 special party conference, televised across the Soviet Union, with delegates openly confronting the *nomenklatura* face-to-face? The success of Gorbachev's reforms will not transform the Soviet Union into either a Western-style democracy or a Scandanavian-type welfare state. But the political trajectory of the Soviet Union does appear to be headed toward a hybrid authoritarian state-capitalist model.

The Soviet Union appears increasingly a status quo power, albeit a heavily armed one with an abiding geopolitical rivalry with the United States. From Gorbachev's moves in the past three years, government policies seem driven more by perceived national interest than by millennial beliefs in the inevitable triumph of socialism. In this context, the Afghan settlement may be the harbinger of new possibilities for managing conflict. Gorbachev has outlined his ideas in an oft-overlooked essay published in September 1987 (in both *Pravda* and *Izvestia,* see Appendix G) on the role of the United Nations and international law in global security. The essay stood many long-standing Soviet notions about the United Nations on their heads. Most immediately, with an eye on both Afghanistan and Cambodia, Gorbachev advocated wider use of UN military observers and UN peacekeeping forces. Moscow has since repaid $223 million in arrears to the United Nations and altered its policy to allow Soviet citizens to become permanent UN civil servants as part of its new effort to increase the effectiveness of the world body.

Gorbachev sketched a range of ambitious proposals to build the United Nations into an instrument to oversee collective security. He suggested, for example, setting up "under the aegis of the UN a mechanism for extensive international verification of compliance with agreements to lessen international tension, limit armaments and to monitor the military situation in conflict areas." Along with more extensive use of UN forces, he proposed that the permanent members become guarantors of regional security. In addition, he advocated strengthening UN agencies, creating a UN space agency, giving the United Nations a role in verifying arms control agreements, establishing institutions for ecological and economic security, and enacting a new human rights code.

The exploratory tone of Gorbachev's article suggests it is conceived less as a specific alternative system of world order than as a missive to provoke debate on a new multilateralism. While some of his proposals appear wildly unrealistic, others serve as a potentially useful point of departure for discussion. In some respects, his ideas evoke the original conception of the United Nations held by the Roosevelt administration. His suggestions for new forms of cooperation with the United States (especially in Asia) imply a different type of superpower relationship that would require vastly different perceptions of Soviet behavior. All vestiges of the Brezhnev era would have to be erased—something still precluded by the present ambiguity of Soviet activities and lingering doubts about the durability of the revised approach.

Many of Gorbachev's Asian arms control proposals still bear traces of Kennan's depiction of Soviet policies as "persistent pressure toward the disruption and weakening of all rival influence and rival power." One could charitably argue that the time lag between the conception and implementation of Gorbachev's "new thinking" on Asia is a product of the Brezhnev legacy rather than questionable Soviet intentions. But that would require an imprudent leap of faith by U.S. policymakers. While there are signs of change in the sources and character of Soviet behavior, Gorbachev's policies still lack permanence, nor are they uniformly different from the past.

A more modest argument could be made that Washington has thus far not explored Gorbachev's myriad proposals, and that what may appear to be classic "zero-sum" initiatives to gain Soviet advantage could be the opening shot of an effort to create improved security relations in Asia. Events such as the INF accord, Afghanistan, and movement on Cambodia do imply a new type of competition with the United States in which the traditional superpower rivalry appears counterproductive. It is also a type of competition in which the United States has yet to seriously test.

· 8 ·
The U.S. Response:
What Is to Be Done?

Gorbachev has clearly answered the question of whether the Soviets intend to be a full-fledged Asia/Pacific power. The answer is yes. Gorbachev seeks to maximize Soviet influence in the world, and that includes Asia. The region is of central importance not only to Gorbachev's foreign policy, but to the success of his economic reforms as well. Gorbachev's low-cost, low-risk, "new look" foreign policy is still barely out of its conceptual stage and has generally attained only a modest reception. But, mingled with other global political and economic trends, it has begun to alter threat perceptions not only in East Asia, but in Western Europe, the Middle East, and even in Latin America. Some of the (actual and potential) receptivity to Soviet overtures in Asia is, in part, a response to poorly orchestrated U.S. foreign and international economic policies. While it is difficult to fault either the basic design or execution of current U.S. foreign policy toward Asia, inadequate coordination with U.S. international economic and trade policies is a source of growing friction, both within the executive branch and between the executive and Congress. For the United States, the difficulty is in synchronizing national security and economic policies, which at times appear to be working at cross purposes. For Asia, such awkward American behavior generates perceptions of retreat, unreliability, and decline. For the Soviets, it creates limited opportunities and openings. (The heavy-handed effort, for example, to force South Korea to open its markets to American cigarettes has generated unnecessary anti-American sentiment, even evoking images of the nineteenth-century opium wars.)[1]

Nonetheless, the basic vitality of the U.S. position in Asia does not seem to be eroding, even as it calls for increasingly skillful management. The incredibly fluid and changing political milieu in the region will require a host of creative adjustments in U.S. policy. The first step in safeguarding U.S. interests is recognizing that the Soviet Union has become a major player on what previously had been an American home court. This dramatically reduces the American margin of error and increases the need for enlightened activism. A complacent or defensive U.S. approach runs the risk of losing the initiative and permitting the Soviets a greater opportunity to shape the political environment.

Unfortunately, much of the U.S. debate about Gorbachev's foreign policy has focused on whether the changes are of a stylistic and tactical nature or whether Gorbachev represents a change in the character of Soviet behavior. The prime force sustaining the continuity in Soviet Asia policy is the Brezhnev legacy. Gorbachev has sought to submerge the military dimension beneath new foundations of political and economic participation, and to obtain Soviet strategic goals through a barrage of arms control proposals rather than through intimidation and coercive diplomacy. Many of Gorbachev's policies, however, remain clouded in ambiguity. Most of the Asia-focused arms control proposals enunciated thus far, for example, would impinge on U.S. military capabilities but would have little substantial effect on Soviet deployments. They appear carefully calculated more for public relations effect than as serious points of departure for a dialogue with the United States. An accord in the START talks would, however, be a way to significantly reduce Asian nuclear deployments by both superpowers and address Asian nuclear fears.

The prerequisite for greater Soviet economic involvement in the Pacific is an economy that is itself more competitive, less protectionist, and more open. This, of course, depends on the success of perestroika. China's experience over the past decade is instructive: as it has implemented market-oriented reforms, it has become increasingly integrated into the world economy. This pattern might be replicated by Moscow. But until its reforms are fulfilled, the somewhat frantic efforts by the Soviets to prove themselves economic players in the region appear more politically motivated than financially expeditious. Their marginal economic involvement in the non-Communist economies of the Pacific renders membership in the Asian Development Bank (ADB) or PECC or other international institutions largely an academic question. But Moscow has gained credence for the idea that the Soviets are entitled to play an economic role, achieving a sense of legitimacy that appears to have been Gorbachev's short-term goal.

Moscow's newly asserted status as a Pacific power is not necessarily a "zero-sum" loss for the United States. The challenge and opportunity for Washington is to help define the terms of Soviet participation. American policymakers should clearly differentiate between genuine strategic threats (such as Soviet aid to the CPP/NPA in the Philippines) and a Soviet political presence—for example, attending ADB meetings, reflagging Kuwaiti tankers—that reflects the new realities of Soviet participation in Asia. Some aspects of Soviet behavior, such as obtaining fishing rights in the Pacific, are more complex, having both a political and strategic component. In Kiribati and Vanuatu, Soviet access offers advantages for its space and satellite operations (controlled by HiTech ships deployed in the region), and for monitoring U.S. missile tests and SDI research in the area.[2]

The basic motivation behind Gorbachev's policy—Soviet weakness and the need for a respite from strategic competition—provides the United States and its allies with the leverage they need to set the price for Soviet economic and political participation in the Pacific Rim. The critical task for the next administration is to fashion a strategy that maximizes the U.S. comparative advantage—in ideological, economic, and political terms—and tests Soviet intentions. Thus far, Washington has been in a largely defensive and reactive mode, failing to offer its own agenda. The architecture of U.S. policy toward Asia should be to construct a framework that sets a series of benchmarks against which to evaluate Soviet behavior. These are the building blocks of a new relationship. Serious U.S. counteroffers to Gorbachev's proposals would allow the United States to regain the political initiative, reduce the Soviet Union's opportunities to expand its influence, and perhaps most importantly, test Soviet sincerity and expose Soviet insincerity.

Again, it is important to stress that this is not a zero-sum game. There are areas where the U.S. objective is not to exploit Soviet weaknesses or profit from Soviet errors, but to preserve existing relationships such as those with Japan, Korea, and the Philippines. Both superpowers have parallel interests—in conventional and nuclear arms control, in reducing tensions, and in regional political stability, as the Afghan accords demonstrated. These provide grounds for cooperation. Similarly, Soviet desires for economic participation offer an opportunity to test the parameters of Moscow's own economic reforms: Do the Soviets want to become a donor to the ADB? Do they want to submit their budget and economic statistics to IMF scrutiny? Do they want to join the GATT enough to reduce protectionism and adopt market-driven price reforms and have a convertible ruble? If they do, there is little reason to oppose their participation in Western economic institutions. Decisions permitting Moscow to join such institutions would not rely on simple trust or faith in Soviet intentions but would result from measurable changes in Soviet behavior.

The guiding principle for the U.S. response to the Soviet challenge in Asia is that each step be part of a coherent U.S. policy that bolsters American advantages, reduces U.S. inconsistencies, and strengthens U.S. relationships with friends and allies in the region. The success of such a comprehensive approach would automatically limit Soviet opportunities.

Some modest proposals for a U.S. agenda might include:

• *Japan.* Reduction of the continuing friction in U.S.-Japanese relations. By any measure, the U.S.-Japanese strategic relationship has reached new plateaus in the 1980s. Similarly, our economies have become so intertwined that it is often difficult to tell where one begins and the other ends. But trade disputes have generated negative undercurrents in the relationship. The current situation is fostering resentment and resulting in destabilizing protectionist/nationalistic responses on both sides of the Pacific. The enormity and complexity of the U.S.-Japanese relationship leave both sides little choice but to sort out differences.

The United States should encourage Japan to: (1) implement the 1986 Maekawa report, which outlined a blueprint for structural reform of the Japanese economy; (2) boost Japan's global economic role. Its foreign aid should be viewed as part of its defense burden, and the total (defense and economic aid) should grow to about 3 percent of Japan's GNP. Japan can meet the defense commitments it has agreed to with no more than 1.5 percent of its GNP. While its economic aid has grown substantially, it is still less than 0.31 percent of its GNP, inadequately administered and insufficiently coordinated with programs of the United States and the IMF/World Bank (particularly in critical areas such as the Philippines). Japan should continue to use its financial power to define a more lucid global political role; (3) enhance Japanese cooperation in science and technology. Tokyo must be more forthcoming in providing the United States with military and dual-use technology as agreed to in the 1983 bilateral accord. In the period ahead, a more equitable partnership in all areas of science and technology is likely to be a critical determinant to maintaining and deepening the U.S.-Japanese alliance.

On the U.S. side, the principal task toward achieving a more balanced relationship with Tokyo is controlling fiscal and monetary policies. The United States must be less self-indulgent and increase savings, reduce consumption, and dramatically reduce its budget deficit. Such domestic policy changes, combined with steady pressure on Japan to open its markets, are key to sustaining a balanced and healthy partnership. Otherwise, U.S. trade tensions with Japan as well as with the East Asian NICs threaten to become unmanageable. One possible initiative would be to establish a Pacific version of the OECD, an Organization of Pacific Trade and Development (OPTAD), as former Prime Minister Nakasone suggested. This would be a multilateral, nonpolitical forum in which to address the problems of the trade regime. In addition to such a pan-Pacific framework, the United States should consider reorganizing its own policy bureaucracy to be better equipped to manage policy. Conflicting objectives between agencies with varying bureaucratic imperatives such as the Commerce Department, United States Trade Representative, State Department, and Department of Defense (not to mention congressional intervention) make for an unwieldy process, often sending mixed signals to Japan and other trading partners. One option might include a Japan Secretariat on the National Security Council with a mandate to coordinate disparate (and sometimes conflicting) elements of trade, finance, technology, and national security policies.

• *China*. Over the past eight years, the U.S.-China relationship has been markedly broadened and institutionalized, building solid foundations in the areas of trade and finance, science and technology exchanges, educational and cultural cooperation, military exchanges, and intelligence cooperation. The United States should nurture these ties and maintain support for China's modernization and still-fragile economic reforms—particularly in the period of leadership transition when Deng Xiaoping passes from the scene.

But China's increasingly assertive "independent foreign policy" suggests redefined limits of Sino-American common interests. The United States should carefully reassess its China policy, clearly delineating the areas of potential policy coordination and points of conflict. Chinese territorial claims in the South China Sea may be a point of conflict. Similarly, Chinese arms sales to Iran and Saudi Arabia, providing them with sophisticated missile systems, mark another area of divergent interests if such policies continue.

The United States should closely monitor the transfer of technology, limiting military sales and military-related technology solely to defensive weapons systems. Technologies that could aid China's nuclear weapons program (including command and control), offensive weapons systems, and electronic warfare capabilities should be withheld both bilaterally and through COCOM. The United States should place an emphasis on bringing China into arms control regime, both in terms of conventional arms transfers and nuclear arms control.

Politically, the United States should refrain from any intervention in the China-Taiwan relationship and reunification dialogue. The United States should increase coordination with China in regard to the Korean Peninsula. The United States should also accelerate the dialogue with China about its Middle East policies.

Economically, the United States should continue to facilitate China's integration into the international trade and finance system. China's pending membership in the GATT should be held to the same standards as those of other nonmarket economies—the adoption of liberalized trade policies, eliminating export subsidies and nontariff barriers.

• *The Philippines.* The Philippines should be a high foreign policy priority. The fragility of its restored democratic institutions, the continuing Communist insurgency, and economic problems require careful management and sensitivity to nascent Philippine nationalism, which is not necessarily anti-American.

Renegotiation of the military bases agreement (MBA) for Clark Air Base and Subic Bay, which expires in 1991, should occur in the larger framework of U.S.-Philippine relations accompanied by vigorous public diplomacy underscoring the regional importance of the bases and the economic and security benefits accruing to the Philippines. ASEAN and Japan should be enlisted in this campaign.

If a new MBA cannot be reached either because Manila desires to terminate the base presence or because the Aquino government demands unrealistic compensation, the United States should work with the Philippines to phase out the U.S. presence in stages, re-creating the essential functions of the bases to the extent possible on U.S.-controlled territory (that is, Guam, Saipan, Tinian, Palau). The critical point is that Asian allies are assured that a retreat from the Philippines does not mean any reduced U.S. commitment to a forward-deployed presence in the Asia/Pacific region.

The United States should take the lead in forming an Intergovernmental Group for the Philippines (IGGP), modeled on the IGGI formed to coordinate aid to Indonesia as the mechanism for increased aid flows. The IGGP, perhaps under the direction of the World Bank, would coordinate aid flows to the Philippines from foreign donors, whom the United States would encourage to increase contributions. Such a strategy would maximize the effectiveness of foreign aid.

The United States should also work with Manila to fashion a program of debt relief for the Philippines' $29 billion foreign debt. Debt relief could be a part of a compensation package for the next base agreement. It could be done on both a bilateral and multilateral basis, with the United States reconsidering Philippine debts to the U.S. government and working out other public- and private-sector debts in coordination with commercial banks and the World Bank. The United States should also explore ways to increase trade and investment in the Philippines.

• *Korea.* The Korean Peninsula remains one of the world's most explosive flashpoints. Here, the interests of the United States, China, the Soviet Union, and Japan all intersect. Barring any further North Korean terrorism, the post-Olympic political climate is such that initiatives are possible at several levels: (1) the United States should encourage North-South Korean dialogue on family visits, culture, and educational exchanges as confidence-building measures, as Seoul has proposed; (2) the United States could begin nonstrategic trade as well as a diplomatic dialogue with the North; (3) in coordination with Moscow and Beijing, the United States should initiate talks for conventional arms reductions on the Korean Peninsula with the understanding that it would ultimately consider reducing or removing its 43,000 troops, in the context of a North-South Korea reconciliation process. In the interim, the United States could restructure command forces, allowing a Korean commander to lead the combined forces; (4) the United States should quietly work more intensely with Moscow and Beijing toward at least informal cross-recognition with the goal of fostering a "two Germanys" solution until reunification becomes a realistic goal.

• *Indochina.* The United States, which has deferred to ASEAN and China in its policy toward Vietnam and Cambodia, should now become more assertive even as it continues a policy of consulting with them. The U.S. economic embargo against Vietnam has become seriously frayed at the edges. Japan, Singapore, Thailand, and South Korea are quietly and increasingly engaging in economic activity with Hanoi.

The United States should fashion a package deal to reach a broader settlement than just Cambodia. The goal would be to provide Vietnam an alternative to its dependence on Moscow. Vietnam would agree to withdraw from Cambodia, to admit a UN peacekeeping force, and to accept a Sihanouk-led coalition government. It would further agree to phase out the Soviet military presence at Cam Ranh Bay and Da Nang

(Moscow could retain base access, but not full-time base facilities) and to resolve POW/MIA issues.

In exchange, the United States could offer Vietnam full normalization of relations, PL480 humanitarian aid, private investment, and support for a multilateral aid package through the World Bank Asian Development Bank. It could also press key donors—France, Japan, Australia—to form an international aid consortium to maximize the flow of resources to Vietnam. And it could urge ASEAN to consider Vietnam for membership perhaps beginning with observer status (provided it curbed its relations with Moscow and implemented economic reforms).

This complex deal would require delicate, quiet diplomacy. But Vietnamese economic reforms suggest that Hanoi's economic imperative is beginning to become as important to them as Soviet reforms are to Gorbachev. This may presage interest in such dramatic movement among the Hanoi leadership. Whether or not such a package deal is a viable option, these objectives—encouraging market-oriented reforms, political and economic movement toward ASEAN, and diluted Vietnamese ties to the Soviets, should guide U.S. policy toward Indochina.

• *Regional Arms Reduction.* In conjunction with START talks to reduce deployments in Asia, a U.S. initiative could explore parallel U.S.-Soviet reductions of conventional and nuclear deployments. The focus of arms control in Asia should continue to be the successful conclusion of a START treaty, combined with aggressive U.S. public diplomacy to explain its rationale. But the United States and USSR could begin to search for a formula that recognized the asymmetry of respective force structures in the region and in relation to overall U.S. and Soviet force structures.

• *Arms Sales.* The United States could seek a multilateral accord with the USSR and China to limit the quantity and quality of arms sales to Third World clients. This could include bringing China and India into a ballistic missile regime.

• *Nuclear-free Zones.* A U.S. initiative could define the terms for nuclear-free zones in East Asia consistent with U.S. interests and military requirements—that is, zones that do not impede or obstruct the transit or docking of U.S. ships and planes. This overture might also include putting pressure on France to cease testing in the South Pacific (and perhaps use Nevada instead) and asking it to cooperate with ASEAN and other regional groups. The United States might reconsider its opposition to the South Pacific Nuclear Free Zone and might have to work with ASEAN to ensure that the ZOPFAN idea does not curtail U.S. deployments.

• *Reduce Superpower Military Activities.* Burgeoning U.S. and Soviet military activities in the Pacific are a growing source of mutual and regional tensions. Washington launched a formal protest when a Soviet SS-18 test-firing landed barely five hundred miles from Hawaii. In 1987 the U.S. Alaskan Air Defense Command intercepted fifty-three Soviet aircraft. The Japanese Air Force scrambled Soviet aircraft 826 times in 1986. According to CINCPAC, the United States conducted forty-six military exercises in East Asia in 1987. Both the United States and the Soviet Union have increasingly become engaged in something of a game of chicken, staging provocative exercises and mock attacks near each other's respective territory.

A number of confidence-building measures to de-escalate tensions in Northeast Asia could be considered: reduce the scope and frequency of military exercises; give better prior notification of exercises and allow either neutral or opposing observer teams; establish hot-line communications between U.S. and Soviet regional commands.

Code of Conduct

Ultimately, Asia could serve as a political laboratory to develop a realistic "code of conduct" for managing superpower relations. The precedents, however, are not encouraging. The agreement on basic principles signed by Nixon and Brezhnev in 1972 foundered on its vagueness (pledges not to seek "unilateral advantages" and Soviet insistence that its support for "national liberation movements" was outside of the equation). In fact, both sides applied double standards when judging the behavior of the other.

Any workable definition of a code of conduct must acknowledge the legitimate interests of each side: if a code precluded Soviet intervention in Africa, it might also preclude U.S. intervention in Grenada. Reciprocity would have to be built into any understanding. Some of Gorbachev's proposals for bolstering the United Nations may serve as a useful starting point for discussion.

Realism would suggest that establishing viable rules of restraint and competition in Asia or the Third World is a long-term proposition. A realistic agenda would avoid grandiose, abstract, and unenforceable goals.

Many of the initiatives discussed above could serve as building blocks for a practical understanding.

During the Nixon-Kissinger period of detente, the United States pressed for an accord defining legitimate conduct. Today, in the still-embryonic neo-detente period we are entering, it is the Soviets who are suggesting it. Any set of understandings agreed to by the United States must test the sincerity of the Soviet challenge. Whether the understandings are a full-blown code of conduct or more limited measures, the objective must be to make Moscow's behavior consistent with Gorbachev's rhetoric.

An American failure to devise constructive initiatives that put Gorbachev's "new thinking" to the test will ensure that Moscow's involvement in the region will occur on its own terms. To the extent that the Soviets seek to compete ideologically, economically, or politically rather than militarily, this should be welcomed: Moscow has little to offer. And to the extent to which the new Soviet diplomacy in Asia is a tactical ruse, a fair-minded U.S. response will only serve to expose it.

In a sense, assessing Gorbachev's still-evolving policy toward Asia and the Pacific at this historical juncture is a bit like shooting at a moving target. Since the first draft of this manuscript was written in March 1988 it has been continually updated and revised to encompass developments through October 1988. The dizzying pace of events has altered neither the broad contours nor the ambiguity of Gorbachev's post-Vladivostok Asia policy. Continuity with the past is illustrated by Moscow's heavy-handed efforts to impose a post-occupation, pro-Soviet regime in Afghanistan, even as its troops are withdrawing. Yet there have also been amazing new twists and turns few would have predicted as recently as the beginning of the year.

Until mid-1988, few would have anticipated a spring 1989 Sino-Soviet summit, Soviet-South Korean official economic (let alone political) relations, the prospect of a Vietnamese withdrawal from Cambodia in 1989, or a Soviet-Japanese summit. Yet all these developments are now unfolding or on the horizon. They are defining events of a new geopolitical milieu in East Asia—one that poses new challenges and offers new opportunities to the incoming administration in Washington, whose response to the new Soviet challenge is likely to figure prominently in the shaping of both East-West relations and the strategic equilibrium of the Pacific.

Appendix Contents

Author's Note: Some appendices have been excerpted in the interest of brevity
and pertinence to the subject matter of the book. In all such cases, entire
passages rather than single words or phrases have been removed. In places
where the act of removing text may affect the reader's perceptions of the
material at hand, omissions have been marked with an ellipsis.

SOVIET UNION

★ Petropavlovsk

Vladivostok ★ ■ KURILE ISLANDS

N. KOREA JAPAN ▲ Misawa P A C I F I C

S. KOREA ▲ Yokosuka

CHINA Kunsan ■

Midway Islands ▲

Okinawa ▲

HONG KONG

TAIWAN ▲ Marcus Island

LAOS VIETNAM Kwajalein

Clark Air Base/Subic Bay ▲

THAILAND ▲

CAM RANH ★ Guam ▲ MICRONESIA

BAY PHILIPPINES

MARSHALL ISLANDS

MALAYSIA NAURU

BRUNEI

SINGAPORE SOLOMON ISLANDS

INDONESIA PAPUA NEW GUINEA

VANUATU

FIJI

INDIAN OCEAN ▲ AUSTRALIA

▲

▲

NEW ZEALAND

▲ U.S. Military Bases and Facilities
★ U.S.S.R. Military Bases and Facilities
■ Major Straits

Appendix A
Map of the Region

Appendix B
Mikhail Gorbachev Talks about International Affairs

Vladivostok. July 28, 1986. TASS.

The realization of the need of peace for everyone is forcefully grasping the minds of the peoples even where the governments continue believing that weapons and war are tools of politics. It (this realization) is precisely for everyone since a nuclear war would not just be a clash between two blocs, two confronting forces. It will lead to a global disaster in which human civilization will be threatened with destruction.

Our initiatives on nuclear disarmament—considerable cuts in the conventional weapons and armed forces, control and the creation of a healthier international atmosphere—were met in different ways.

The friendly countries have expressed support for them. The countries of the socialist community view them, with good reason, as a component part of the general policy of socialism in the world arena. And not only because these initiatives have been coordinated with them, not only for principled internationalist considerations, but also because both we and they are engaged in a purely peaceful effort—the refinement of our societies. The salutary process of drawing closer is being intensified on this basis, economic integration is taking on a wider scope, concrete steps are being made to create joint factories and amalgamations, and active human contacts are being broadened.

In a word, a progressive, mutually beneficial process extending cooperation and fraternity among the peoples of the community is under way.

The developing world shows much interest in our plans and intentions—both internal and international ones. We note that many developing countries wish to expand and deepen further economic, scientific and cultural cooperation with the Soviet Union. We are prepared for that.

It would be fair to say that the Western public at large and representatives of the business world who have a realistic view of things, who do not suffer

104

from anticommunist paranoia and do not associate themselves with profits from the arms race, regard our plans seriously, with interest. They also stand for peace and cooperation, for the development of healthy economic, scientific and cultural ties with the Soviet Union. We welcome such an approach.

Yet, in many capitalist countries the fashion, as before, is set by forces whose past and future are blinded by animosity toward socialism, by imperial ambitions or are firmly geared to the war business. But the latter is known to be extremely voracious and ruthless. Yesterday it needed millions, today it needs billions, and tomorrow it will need trillions. It will never start manufacturing, of its own free will, toys for children instead of missiles since this is in its nature.

The ruling circles of the United States and some countries allied to it are trying either to characterize our peace initiatives as sheer propaganda or allege that only the Soviet Union stands to gain from them. Yes, we stand to gain from disarmament, even if this term is used, just as all peoples and governments who now spend billions on the arms race stand to gain from disarmament. Yet it is only a part of the truth.

I will even say, a smaller part of the truth. The main truth is that our initiatives stem from profound concern about mankind's destiny.

It is absurd and criminal to act in the face of a nuclear threat according to an old, already dead scheme: What is good for the socialist countries should be rejected. Clearly visible in that is the class narrow-mindedness, the primitive, ideological, mechanical approach, the growing political influence of militarism. Yet I am not inclined to believe that the military-industrial complex is all-powerful. We see that the world public ever more clearly realizes the danger of militarism. We see that, despite permanent chauvinistic indoctrination, realistic sentiments are growing in the United States. The realization is deepening that the source of the military threat to the United States is not the Soviet people, not the socialist countries, not the peasants of Nicaragua, not the faraway Vietnamese or Libyans, but its own arms manufacturers and irresponsible politicians serving them, the adventurist militarists.

We certainly understand that the ruling forces of imperialism are seriously concerned about the international influence of our plans designed for accelerated socioeconomic and scientific-technical development. We also know that the arms race, which is gaining momentum, serves not only the aim of superprofits and preparations for war, but other immoral aims as well, whose essence is to exhaust the Soviet Union economically, to frustrate the party's course for a further rise in the living standards of the people, to hamper the implementation of the social program. We also know precisely who continues cherishing the hope for a planned, methodical destruction of the USSR and of the socialist countries, using economic, moral-psychological, propaganda, political and military methods to that end.

This is a futile effort. The time has come to reckon with the realities rather than to make policy on the basis of illusions and misconceptions.

If there are no treaties, this will not bring relief to the world, there will be no tranquility. Fear will not disappear until some rulers in the West give up the dangerous attempts, which are, perhaps, consoling for them but are fruitless, to put the Soviet Union on its knees, splitting the socialist community and hampering our forward progress.

The time persistently demands a new understanding of the present stage in the development of civilization, of international relations, of the world. This is a controversial and complex world, but it is objectively united by the bonds of interdependence—international relations under which, despite all the differences and clashes of interest, one can no longer live under the ancient traditions of "the law of the fist," a civilization demonstrating the unprecedented strength of the human mind and labor and, simultaneously, its fragility, vulnerability on the part of the forces released by human genius but placed at the service of destruction.

All this dictates the need for and makes urgent a radical breaking of many customary attitudes to foreign policy, a breaking of the traditions of political thinking, of views on problems of war and peace, on defense, the security of individual states and international security. In this connection it is clear that our radical and global, in the full sense of the word, proposals such as the program for the elimination, by the end of this century, of nuclear and other mass destruction weapons, a total ban on nuclear weapons testing, a ban on chemical weapons, programs for cooperation in the peaceful uses of outer space and a whole number of others concern the whole world, all countries.

The main problem confronting humankind today—that of survival—is equally acute and urgent for Europe, Africa, America and Asia. Yet in each part of the world it looks different. Therefore, while staying here, in Vladivostok, it is natural to look at international policy issues from the Asian-Pacific viewpoint.

Such an approach is justified for many reasons. In the first place, because east of the Urals—in Asia, in Siberia, in the Far East—lies the largest part of our country's territory. It is here that many national tasks put forward by the party congress will be resolved. Hence, the situation in the Far East as a whole, in Asia and the ocean expanses washing it, where we have been permanent inhabitants and seafarers of long standing, is to us of national and state interest.

Many major states of the world, including the USSR, the United States, India, China, Japan, Vietnam, Mexico and Indonesia, are situated on the enormous expanses of this territory spreading over almost half of the Earth. Here lie states which are considered to be medium-size ones, but are rather large by European standards—Canada, the Philippines, Australia and New Zealand—and along with them there are dozens of comparatively smaller and tiny countries. Some of them have a history of many thousands of years or many centuries, others have formed in modern times, and still others have formed quite recently.

Asia, which woke up to a new life in the twentieth century, has enriched world progress with its diversified and unique experience in the fight for freedom and independence. This is not only history. This is a living legacy making up one of the important fundamentals of the current political realities in this part of the world.

Every country has its own social and political system with every thinkable variation, its own traditions, achievements and difficulties, its own way of life and beliefs, convictions and prejudices, its own understanding of spiritual and material values. Each of them has something to be proud of and something to uphold in the treasure house of human civilization.

This impressive diversity, this colossal human and sociopolitical massif calls for appropriate attention, study and respect. We know well from our own Soviet experience what an immense creative force the revived sense of national dignity becomes, what a constructive role is played by the national identity of a people in its organic interrelationship with other equal and free peoples. This process is on the rise in Asia and the Pacific now: Everything is in motion here, far from everything has settled. The new is mixing with the old, a way of life which seemed unshakable only yesterday is giving way to the whirlwind of change—social, scientific and technical, and ideological. This is, I would say, yet another period of renaissance in world history, a period harboring a huge potential of progress. And this is true not only with regard to Asia and Oceania.

Which way will socioeconomic and political development take? What processes will prevail in the inter-state relations? These issues will largely determine the destiny of the entire world.

Socialism is an inalienable factor of the large-scale and complex changes in this region. It gained firm positions in Asia as a result of the Great October Revolution and the victory over fascism and Japanese militarism, as a result of the great Chinese Revolution, after the new social system was consolidated in Mongolia and on Korean land, whose people displayed outstanding steadfastness in the struggle for the socialist future of their country, and then in Vietnam and Laos. But it is also in Asia where it was confronted with the most brutal and cynical counteraction. Vietnam is the most graphic example. Its heroic experience, the lessons of its victory over imperialism highlighted again the irresistible strength of the ideas of freedom and socialism.

This region, Asia, saw the formation of the concept of nonalignment, a movement which now includes more than a hundred nations. It is seeking to come up with its own response to the challenge of the times, is actively working for overcoming the world's division into military blocs and is looking for ways to diminish the nuclear threat. In rejecting and condemning exploitation, the policy of aggression and neocolonialism, the Nonaligned Movement is urging mankind toward unity, toward cooperation in combating hunger and the glaring poverty of hundreds of millions of people.

The great India, with its moral authority and traditional wisdom, and its specific political experience and huge economic potential, is the recognized leader of this movement. We highly assess its contribution to asserting standards of equitable coexistence and justice in the international community. Friendly relations between the USSR and India became a stabilizing factor on a worldwide scale.

Japan has turned into a power of front-rank importance. The country which became the first victim of American nuclear weapons covered a great distance within a brief period, demonstrated striking accomplishments in industry, trade, education, science and technology. These successes are due not only to the self-control, discipline and energy of the Japanese people, but also due to "three nonnuclear principles" which officially underlie its international policy, although lately—and this must be emphasized—they, as well as the peaceful provisions of Japan's Constitution, are being circumvented more openly.

But we also see many other things in Asia and Oceania. The peoples' dignity, insulted by colonialism, the legacy of poverty, illiteracy and backwardness, along with profound prejudices, preserve conditions for mistrust and hostility between peoples, including those living within one state. Imperialism speculates on the difficulties and prejudices, which brings about local conflicts, ethnic and religious strife and political instability.

Whenever independence becomes a tangible international value and there emerges a threat to the exploiter interests of imperialism, it resorts to its favorite methods: economic blackmail, intrigues and plots against the leadership of the country in question and interference in internal problems. It maintains separatists and finances and even directly arms counterrevolution and terrorists. Punjab, the Tamil problem, where attempts are being made to turn this one against India too, the undeclared wars on Kampuchea and Afghanistan, the annexation of Micronesia, interference in the Philippines and pressure on New Zealand offer enough examples to see how the contemporary mechanism of imperialist intervention and diktat operates.

The experience of history, the laws of growing interdependence and the integration requirements of the economy call us to look for ways to unify and establish open ties between nations within the region and beyond it. These nations have tens, hundreds of arduous problems inherited from the colonial past and emerging out of the contradictions of present-day development. And they are being dragged into blocs, while the freedom of handling their own resources is being curtailed. They are being forced to inflate their military budgets, are being swept into the arms race, and their economy and entire social life is being militarized.

All this subverts the processes of internal development, generates tension and, naturally, stands in the way of normalizing relations between nationalities and states.

The Soviet Union is also an Asian and Pacific country. It realizes the complex problems of this vast region. It is directly contiguous to them. This is what determines the balanced and overall view of this giant part of the world with a mass of diverse nations and peoples. Our approach to it is based on the recognition and understanding of the existing realities.

At the same time our interest is not a claim to privileges and special position, are [sic] not egoistic attempts to strengthen our security at someone else's expense and is not a search for benefit to others' detriment. Our interest is in the pooling of efforts and in cooperation, with full respect for each people's right to live as they choose and resolve their problems on their own in conditions of peace.

We are in favor of building together new, fair relations in Asia and the Pacific.

Recently, I had many meetings with leaders of European nations, with various political figures of European countries. Involuntarily, I compare the situation in Asia with that in Europe.

The Pacific region has not yet been militarized to the extent this has taken place in Europe. But the potential for its militarization is truly immense, and the consequences are extremely dangerous. A glance at the map will convince one of that. Major nuclear powers are situated here. Powerful land armies, mighty navies and air forces have been established. The scientific, technological and industrial potential of many countries—from the western to the eastern fringes of the ocean—makes it possible to boost any arms race. The situation is being exacerbated by the preservation of conflict situations. Let us not forget: It was in Asia that American imperialism waged the two biggest wars since 1945—in Korea and Indochina. One can hardly count even several years during the past four decades where the flames of war were not blazing in one or another part of the Asian and Pacific region.

In Europe, the Helsinki process of dialogue, talks and agreements is in operation, sometimes effectively, sometimes not so effectively. This brings a certain stability and reduces the probability of armed conflicts. In the region in question, this is absent or nearly absent. If something has been changing lately, it has not been for the better. Since the second half of the seventies, the U.S. has undertaken large-scale measures to build up armed forces in the Pacific Ocean. The militarized "triangle" of Washington, Tokyo and Seoul is being set up under its pressure. And although two out of three nuclear powers in the region—the People's Republic of China and the USSR—pledged not to be the first to use nuclear weapons, the United States has deployed nuclear weapon-delivery vehicles and nuclear warheads in one of the zones of crisis—the Korean peninsula—and nuclear weapon-delivery vehicles on Japanese territory.

One has to state that militarization and the escalation of the threat of war in this part of the world are picking up dangerous speed. The Pacific Ocean is turning into an arena of military-political confrontation. This is what gives rise to growing concern among the peoples living here. This is alarming also for us from all viewpoints, including for considerations of security in the Asian part of our country.

The Asian and Pacific part of the Soviet Union's foreign policy is an integral part of the overall platform of the CPSU's international activity, worked out by the April Plenary Meeting and the Twenty-seventh Congress. But a platform is not a chart that can be applied to any situation. It is, rather, a set of principles and a method relying on experience.

Proceeding from this, how will it be possible to perceive the process of shaping international security and peaceful cooperation in this vast region?

First of all, in keeping with its principled policy, the Soviet Union will seek to lend dynamism to its bilateral relations with all countries situated here without exception. We shall strengthen friendship in all ways and invigorate our different relations with the Mongolian People's Republic, the Democratic People's Republic of Korea, the Socialist Republic of Vietnam, the People's Democratic Republic of Laos and the People's Republic of Kampuchea. We regard relations with our friends, built on the principles of equality and solidarity, as an integral part of overall Asian and Pacific security. At present, for instance, the question of withdrawing a substantial number of Soviet troops from Mongolia is being examined jointly with the Mongolian leadership.

We are prepared to expand ties with Indonesia, Australia, New Zealand, the Philippines, Thailand, Malaysia, Singapore, Burma, Sri Lanka, Nepal, Brunei, the Republic of Maldives and the youngest independent participants in the region's political life. With some of the latter—Papua New Guinea, Western Samoa, the Kingdom of Tonga, Fiji, the Republic of Kiribati, the Republic of Nauru, Tuvalu and the Republic of Vanuatu—we already maintain diplomatic relations.

Speaking in a city which is only a step from the People's Republic of China, I would like to dwell on the most important issues in our relations. Relations are extremely important for several reasons, starting from the fact that we are neighbors, that we share the world's longest land border and that we, our children and grandchildren are destined to live near each other "forever and ever."

But the question is not, of course, just that. History entrusted the Soviet and the Chinese peoples with an extremely important mission. Much in international development depends on these two major socialist nations.

A noticeable improvement occurred in our relations in recent years. I would like to reaffirm: The Soviet Union is prepared—at any time and at any level—to discuss with China questions of additional measures for creating an atmosphere of goodneighborliness. We hope that the border dividing (I would prefer to say linking) us will become a line of peace and friendship in the near future.

The Soviet people's attitude to the objective advanced by the Communist Party of China—to modernize the country and in the future build a socialist society worthy of a great people—is that of understanding and respect.

As far as it is possible to judge, we have similar priorities with China—those of accelerating social and economic development. Why not support each other, why not cooperate in implementing our plans wherever this will clearly benefit both sides? The better the relations, the more we shall be able to exchange our experience.

We note with satisfaction that a positive shift has become visible in economic ties. We are convinced that the historically established complementarity between the Soviet and the Chinese economies offers great opportunities for expanding these ties, in the border regions as well. Some of the major problems of cooperation are literally knocking at the door. For instance, we do not want the border river of Amur to be viewed as a "water obstacle." Let the basin of this mighty river unite the efforts of the Chinese and the Soviet peoples in using the rich resources available there to our mutual benefit and for building water management projects. An intergovernmental agreement on this account is being jointly worked out, and the official border could pass along the main shipping channel.

The Soviet Government is preparing a positive reply in respect to the issue of assistance in building a railroad to connect the Xinjiang Uygur Autonomous Region with Kazakhstan.

We suggested cooperation with the PRC in space exploration, which could include the training of Chinese cosmonauts. There are great opportunities for mutually beneficial exchanges in the spheres of culture and education. We are prepared, and sincerely want all this.

On relations with Japan. There are emerging signs of a turn for the better here as well. It would be good if the turn did take place. The objective position of our two countries in the world demands profound cooperation on a sound, realistic basis, in a calm atmosphere free from the problems of the past. A beginning was made this year. The foreign ministers exchanged visits. On the agenda is an exchange of top-level visits.

Economic cooperation is of mutual interest. The point at issue is, first of all, our coastal regions, which already have business contacts with Japanese firms. It is possible to discuss the question of establishing joint enterprises in adjacent and nearby regions of the USSR and Japan. Why not establish long-term cooperation in the investigation and comprehensive use of the ocean's resources? Why not link up the programs concerning the peaceful study and use of outer space? The Japanese, it seems, have a method of making relations more dynamic, called "economic diplomacy." Let it serve Soviet-Japanese cooperation this time.

In the Pacific region, the Soviet Union also shares a border with the United States. It is our next-door neighbor in the literal sense of the word, with only seven kilometers dividing us—the exact distance between the Soviet island of Big Diomede and the American island of Little Diomede.

We clearly realize that the U.S. is a great Pacific power, primarily because a considerable part of the country's population lives on the shores of this ocean. The western part of America, gravitating toward this area, is playing a growing part in the country's life and is showing dynamism. Besides, the United States undoubtedly has important, legitimate economic and political interests in the region.

No doubt, without the U.S., without its participation, it is impossible to resolve the problem of security and cooperation in the Pacific Ocean in a way that would satisfy all nations in the region. So far, regrettably, Washington has not shown interest in this; it is not even considering a serious talk on the subject of the Pacific. If this subject is taken up, it leads to the trodden path of the "Soviet threat" and to saber-rattling to corroborate the myth.

Our approach to relations with the U.S. is well known. We stand for peaceful, good-neighborly relations, for mutually beneficial cooperation which has, incidentally, considerable opportunities in the Far East and in the Pacific also.

Talking about the U.S., here are a few words about the most important thing in our relations for the present—the termination of the arms race. After the Geneva meeting the Soviet Union put forward many large-scale proposals on the entire range of problems of reducing and eliminating arms and of verifying the process. We did not see any movement to meet us half-way. We were treated, in point of fact, to the same stuff as prior to the Geneva summit.

With a view to overcoming the marking of time, we went farther along the road toward the USA: New, large-scale compromise proposals were put forward in my June letter to the President of the United States. While visiting here, I received a reply from President Reagan. The reply sets one thinking. We have begun to study it. We shall treat it with responsibility and attention. To us the most important thing is, first of all, the extent to which the proposals contained in the letter meet the principle of equal security and whether they make it possible to reach effective joint solutions in the field of ending the arms race and preventing its spreading over into outer space. We shall determine our further steps accordingly. As far as a new Soviet-U.S. summit meeting is concerned, I can repeat: We favor such a meeting. But we resolutely oppose the interpretation of the accords reached at the previous meeting in Geneva being reduced to the promise to have more meetings. No, the main thing on which we agreed last time with President Reagan and what we signed is the consent to strive for the normalization of relations between the USSR and the USA and for the improvement of the international situation, and to speed up the course of talks on the reduction of armaments. A new summit meeting, too, is called upon to promote that.

We frequently hear from abroad all kinds of inventions to the effect that the Soviet Union is building up its military power in the east of the country. Let me state with all authority: We are not doing anything and shall not do anything over and above the level that corresponds to the minimal requirements of our defense, the defense of our friends and allies, especially in light of the American military activity not far from our and their frontiers.

This applies in full measure to the medium-range missiles. Those who do not want to see world tensions lessening continue to argue that we allegedly will be able to move our SS-20 missiles from the West to the East and from the East to the West. This is why I emphasize one more time—we suggest that both American and Soviet medium-range missiles in Europe be eliminated. Precisely eliminated, and not moved somewhere. It is quite clear that this promotes the interests of Asian countries as well.

I would also like to state that the Soviet Union is a confirmed advocate of disbanding the military groupings, renouncing the possession of military bases in Asia and the Pacific Ocean and withdrawing troops from the territories of other countries. The USSR is a member of the Warsaw Treaty Organization, but it is the European defensive alliance and it operates strictly within the geographical framework determined by the Warsaw Treaty. In our turn we are strongly opposed to U.S. attempts at extending NATO's "competence" to the entire world, including Asia and the Pacific Ocean.

Our views about security in the Asian-Pacific region have not come out of thin air. They take account of the experience of the past and modern times. The principles of "Pancha Shila" and of Bandung have not sunk into oblivion. The positive examples of the truce in Korea, the 1954 Geneva meeting on Indochina, the Indo-Pakistani agreement in Tashkent live on in diplomatic experience. Nowadays, too, we see the efforts of a number of states to solve in practice common economic problems and attempts at settling conflicts one way or another. There is no small amount of things positive in the activities of the ASEAN and in bilateral ties. After the plan for a "Pacific community" had been rejected, discussion of the idea of "Pacific economic cooperation" began. We approached it without bias, and we are ready to join in the deliberations on the possible foundations of such cooperation, of course, if it is conceived not following a bloc-oriented, antisocialist pattern imposed by someone but as a result of a free discussion without any discrimination whatsoever. A sufficiently vast arsenal of scientific and political ideas on the issue of establishing a new world economic order and the experience of integration in the West and the East could become a solid foundation for such discussions.

By way of an objective, no matter if it is a rather remote one, we would propose a conference, in the mold of the Helsinki Conference, to be attended by all the countries gravitating toward the ocean. When an agreement is reached on its convocation (if at all, of course), it will be possible to come to terms on the venue for it. One of the options is Hiroshima. Why shouldn't that city, the first victim of nuclear evil, become the "Helsinki" of sorts for Asia and the Pacific Ocean?

Summing up, I would like to emphasize that we stand for integrating the Asian-Pacific region into the general process of establishing a comprehensive system of international security proposed at the Twenty-seventh Congress of the CPSU.

How do we see it concretely?

First of all, the issues of regional settlement speak for themselves. I'll speak of Afghanistan separately. Now let me talk about Southeast Asia and Kampuchea. The Khmer people sustained terrible losses. That country, its cities and villages came under American bombing raids more than once. With its suffering it has gained the right to choose friends and allies for itself. It is impermissible to try and draw it back into the tragic past, to decide the future of that state in distant capitals or even in the United Nations.

Here, like in other problems of Southeast Asia, much depends on the normalization of Sino-Vietnamese relations. It is a sovereign matter of the governments and the leadership of both countries. We can only express our interest in seeing the border between these socialist states again becoming a border of peace and good-neighborly relations, in seeing comradely dialogue resumed and the unnecessary suspicion and mistrust removed. It seems that the moment is good and that all of Asia needs that.

In our opinion, there are no insurmountable obstacles in the way of establishing mutually acceptable relations between the countries of Indochina and ASEAN. Given goodwill and on the condition of nonintervention from outside, they could solve their problems which would benefit simultaneously the cause of security in Asia.

There is a possibility not only to lessen dangerous tensions in the Korean peninsula but also to start to move along the road of solving the national problem of the entire Korean people. As far as really Korean interests are concerned, there are no sensible reasons for evading the serious dialogue proposed by the Democratic People's Republic of Korea.

Second, we stand for putting up a barrier in the way of the proliferation and buildup of nuclear weapons in Asia and the Pacific Ocean.

As is known, the USSR pledged itself not to increase the number of medium-range nuclear missiles in the Asian part of the country.

The USSR supports proclaiming the southern part of the Pacific a nuclear-free zone and urges all nuclear powers to guarantee its status in unilateral or multi-lateral way.

The implementation of the proposal of the DPRK for the creation of a nuclear-free zone in the Korean peninsula would be a serious contribution. Well-deserved attention was aroused by the idea of creating such a zone in Southeast Asia.

Third, we propose starting talks on the reduction of the activity of fleets in the Pacific, above all nuclear-armed ships. Restriction of the rivalry in the sphere of antisubmarine weapons, specifically, the arrangement to curtail antisubmarine activity in certain zones of the Pacific would help strengthen stability. This could become a substantial confidence-building measure. In general, I would like to say that if the United States gave up military presence, say, in the Philippines, we would not leave this step unanswered.

We remain strongly in favor of resuming the talks on turning the Indian Ocean into a peace zone.

Fourth, the Soviet Union attaches much importance to the radical reduction of armed forces and conventional armaments in Asia to the limits of reasonable sufficiency. We realize that this problem should be tackled gradually, stage-by-stage, starting in one area, say, the Far East. In this context the USSR is prepared to discuss with the PRC concrete steps aimed at proportionate lowering of the level of land forces.

Fifth, the Soviet Union holds that the time has long come to switch the discussion of confidence-building measures and the non-use of force in the region to a practical plane. A start could be made with the simpler measures, for instance, measures for the security of sea lanes in the Pacific, and for the prevention of international terrorism.

A conference to discuss and work out such measures could be held in one of the Soviet maritime cities. By the way, with time the question of opening Vladivostok to visits by foreigners could be solved. If a change for the better in the situation in the Pacific is really achieved, Vladivostok could become one of the major international centers, a commercial and cultural center, a city for festivals, sports events, congresses and scientific symposiums. We would like it to be our wide open window on the East. And the words of our great Pushkin "The ships of every flag and nation will hail our shores" will then apply also to Vladivostok.

And in conclusion, about Afghanistan. It was declared from the rostrum of the Twenty-seventh Congress of the CPSU that we are ready to bring home the Soviet troops stationed in Afghanistan at the request of its government. As you know, the party now firmly adheres to the principle that words should be confirmed by deeds.

Having thoroughly assessed the situation that is shaping and having held consultations with the Government of the Democratic Republic of Afghanistan, the Soviet leadership has adopted a decision which I officially announce today: Six regiments will be brought home from Afghanistan before the end of 1986—one armored regiment, two motorized rifle regiments and three anti-aircraft artillery regiments to the areas of their permanent deployment in the Soviet Union and in such a way that all those who take an interest in this could easily ascertain this.

Taking so serious a step, of which we informed the states concerned, including Pakistan, in advance, the Soviet Union is striving to speed up political settlement, to give it another impetus. The Soviet Union also proceeds from the view that those who organize and implement the armed intervention against the Democratic Republic of Afghanistan will rightly understand and duly appreciate this unilateral step of ours. It must be answered by the curtailment of outside interference in the affairs of the Democratic Republic of Afghanistan.

Certain progress has been achieved of late at the Afghan-Pakistani talks held through the mediation of a representative of the United Nations' Secretary-General. As soon as political settlement is finally worked out, the return of all Soviet troops from Afghanistan can be sped up. Schedules for their stage-by-stage return have been agreed upon with the Afghan leadership.

But all who encourage and finance the undeclared war against Afghanistan and from whose territory it is waged should know that if the intervention against the DRA continues, the Soviet Union will stand up for its neighbor. This stems from our internationalist solidarity with the Afghan people and from the interests of the Soviet Union's security.

We support the line of the present Afghan leadership after national reconciliation, for the widening of the social base of the April national-democratic revolution, including the creation of a government with the participation in it of those political forces that found themselves beyond the country's boundaries but are prepared to participate sincerely in the nationwide process of the construction of a new Afghanistan.

Comrades, this generation inherited many difficult, painful problems. In order to advance to their solution, it is necessary to get rid of the burden of the past, to seek new approaches, guiding oneself by the responsibility for the present and future.

The Soviet state calls on all Asian and Pacific nations to cooperate for the sake of peace and security. Everyone who is striving for these goals, who hopes for a better future for their peoples, will find us to be benevolent interlocutors and honest partners.

Mankind is living through a difficult, dramatic time. But it has a reserve of strength which allows it not simply to survive but also to learn to live in a new, civilized world, in other words, to live without the threat of war, in conditions of freedom, when the benefit of man and the maximum development of the possibilities of a personality will be the highest criterion. But this requires a persistent struggle against the common enemy—the threat of universal destruction.

Mobilization of the potential of common sense existing in the world, [and] the partnership of reason, are now more important than ever to arrest the slide toward catastrophe. Our resolve to do our utmost for this remains unchanged. Everybody can be sure of this.

Appendix C
Soviet Government Statement

Pravda April 24, 1986

The world is passing through an untranquil and crucial phase of development where political will, a new approach, farsighted decisions and practical actions are required to improve the international situation radically. The time now is such that it is necessary to learn the great art of living together in the world as a whole and in individual regions in particular.

Advocating detente, the complete elimination of nuclear weapons before the end of the current century, the building of an all-embracing system of international security and development of cooperation—these proposals have found vivid representation in the documents of the 27th Congress of the Communist Party of the Soviet Union—the USSR takes into full consideration the interests of the countries of the Asia-Pacific region. Important processes are taking place there which cannot but have an impact on the position of the Soviet Union as one of the largest Asian and Pacific powers, on the positions of its friends and allies, and on the interests of international peace and security.

In the existing conditions it is especially vital to show mutual restraint, refrain from any actions that might worsen the political climate in that region of the world and might hold back the consolidation and development of the positive processes there, processes that promote the continuation of dialogue and the search for ways of improving the international situation.

Meanwhile, actions of this kind leading to the aggravation of tensions in the region are being taken by the United States of America and its allies. Judging by everything, certain political circles in the USA and Japan do not picture the future of the Asia-Pacific region in any other way than in the form of confrontation of different countries. On the practical plane, attempts are being made for that purpose to create a structure and mechanism for a so-called "Pacific

Community" to be transformed in the future into a closed regional grouping, into another militarist bloc.

Approaching in the most selective manner the list of potential members of the "Pacific Community," its initiators clearly show no concern for making the proposed organization a truly representative forum for discussion and solution of the long-pressing economic problems of the region, or for changing the inequitable structure of interstate trade and economic relations that has taken shape there.

The world has witnessed more than once how the screen of economic assistance and economic cooperation, and objective processes of internationalization and integration of the world economy have been used to further and substantiate imperialist plans for the establishment of military groupings, "treaties on combined defence" and so forth.

In the opinion of the Soviet government, if no check is made to such a course of events in an area where the interests of many states converge and intertwine, there may be a serious aggravation of tensions in the Asia-Pacific region.

The foundation for friendly relations, for building confidence and promoting mutual understanding among peoples in that part of the world, just as in other regions for that matter, can and should be development of equitable cooperation open to all, rather than efforts to put some states in opposition to others. Given such an approach—and all nations are interested in precisely this—there can be no room for knocking together blocs and counterblocs, for establishing all kinds of "axes," "triangles" and closed groupings, or cultivating protectionism and discriminatory measures in mutual trade and economic ties.

The Soviet government believes that, despite differences in political systems, ideologies and world outlooks, the nations of the Asia-Pacific region are bound together by the community of vital interests. In the conditions of the growing interdependence of states it is much more difficult, or altogether impossible, to solve the existing problems on one's own or in an isolated group; for that purpose it is essential to pool the constructive efforts of all states of the region, irrespective of their socio-political systems.

The elimination of nuclear and chemical weapons by the end of the current century and the prevention of militarization of space, as proposed by the Soviet Union, would rid all nations in the world and, naturally, in the Asia-Pacific region, of the nuclear and chemical threat, radically change the situation, elevate the security of states to a new level, and promote felicitous conditions for mutually advantageous cooperation.

The Soviet Union also proposes to press, through bilateral and multilateral consultations, for a solution to outstanding issues, for better mutual understanding and for building confidence, and thereby to create prerequisites for a pan-Asian forum to jointly seek constructive solutions. It would be possible appropriately to prepare and hold a separate meeting of the countries of the Pacific areas to consider issues of security, including the economic aspect. Considering the potential of the countries of the Pacific area in the political and economic fields, such a meeting—and it should be seen to bring important results—would be a major event for the region and would have a fruitful effect on the situation in the world as a whole.

The implementation of confidence-building measures and a reduction in the activity of navies in the Pacific would play a stabilizing role. The Soviet Union would welcome the establishment of nuclear-free zones in the Asia-Pacific region. The decision of the Southern Pacific countries to declare the area a nuclear-free zone has evoked the most positive response in the Soviet Union.

It stands to reason that all countries of the Pacific area wishing to take part in the consideration of security issues in the Pacific and in the elaboration of decisions should do so. A number of countries have already come forward with various proposals for consolidating security in the area. The proposals deserve serious attention.

In tackling large-scale goals for accelerating social and economic development, the Soviet Union gives paramount attention to Siberia and the Soviet Far East which are part of the Asia-Pacific region. Stable mutually beneficial trade and economic relations have developed between the Soviet Union and many countries in the region. The growth of the industrial and agricultural base, completion of the Baikal-Amur Mainline, development of rich oil-and-gas, coal and other energy resources, and the drawing of new raw timber resources of the area into economic use objectively create additional important material prerequisites for more active USSR participation in the international division of labour, and trade and economic, scientific and technological cooperation with countries in Asia and the Pacific.

The Soviet Union is proposing to start a wide exchange of views between all interested countries of that part of the world on issues aimed at establishing equitable, mutually beneficial and steady trade-and-economic, technological, scientific and cultural cooperation. The following could become spheres for such cooperation: development of productive forces, training of personnel, use of new sources of energy, including nuclear energy, upgrading of means of transportation and communication, discovering of new forms of trade, economic and financial cooperation, with due regard for the interests of the developing countries of the region, exchanges of scientific and technological information, development of measures for the protection of the environment and for the rational use of biological and mineral resources of seas and oceans, peaceful space research in common interests, joint work in the field of medicine and health care, efforts to combat natural calamities and to eliminate their aftermath, and so on.

It is clear that these complex, diverse and large-scale problems will require collective preparation of major long-term projects and programmes, and participation of all countries concerned in their implementation. The ideas which are available in this respect could be considered within the existing UN framework, and through the Economic and Social Commission for Asia and the Pacific in particular.

There is deep conviction in the Soviet Union that the establishment of large-scale cooperation on a basis of equality and mutual benefit of all countries of the Asia-Pacific region, irrespective of the difference in their social systems, meets the basic interests of the countries of that part of the world and will promote a restructuring of international relations on an equitable, democratic basis. Our country is ready to participate most actively in such regional peaceful cooperation and to use for such purposes all the economic, scientific and technological potential at its disposal.

The strengthening of good-neighbourliness and friendship between all Asia-Pacific countries and the pooling of their efforts in a common search for constructive solutions to the security issues in Asia and the Pacific areas would have a favorable effect not only for the Asia-Pacific region but would mark a contribution to the cause of preservation and consolidation of universal peace.

Appendix D
Indonesian Paper Interviews Gorbachev on Arms Control

Merdeka, July 21, 1987.

B. M. Diah: We devote a very great deal of attention to your utterances and to those processes which are taking place in the Soviet Union.

M. S. Gorbachev: Thank you. Have our words "Glasnost" and "Perestroyka" reached you? Are they translated into the Indonesian language?

B. M. Diah: Those words are well known at home, and they need no translation.

M. S. Gorbachev: We have tried to look at the modern world from strictly scientific and realistic stances. The analysis made led us to a new vision of the world and to a new policy which we proclaimed at our party congress. The analysis helped us also to see those realities which characterize the present world. And it differs substantially from how it was 30-40 years ago.

Above all, in connection with the accumulation of enormous stocks of nuclear weapons, human civilization has found itself in jeopardy. This is a reality which has to be reckoned with. Moreover, the correct evaluation of this reality leads on to the conclusion that it is impossible today to resolve problems of world politics militarily. Such a path would be fraught with unpredictable consequences. This means that it is necessary to make adjustments to views of the world and to the policy of the states.

The problems which exist in the world require all countries to pool their efforts. And in general, if one looks at the progress of science and technology, it is bringing us ever more closely together and is linking us more closely than ever. We are increasingly dependent on each other, and we are becoming essential to one another.

B. M. Diah: And, as I recall, you expressed this very idea in your speech in Vladivostok. . . .

Question: We are coming up to the anniversary of your speech in Vladivostok, in which you put forward broad proposals for strengthening peace and security in the Asian and Pacific region. Many events have taken place in this vast region since then. Do you perceive any positive trends in their development?

Answer: I can answer immediately: Yes, I do.

The year that has elapsed and the main events during that year, including our talks with Prime Minister Rajiv Gandhi of India convinced us even more of the correctness and timeliness of raising the questions of security in the Asian and Pacific region. Our approach toward the quest for their solution—being open to a democratic discussion of any ideas and proposals—has also proven correct.

What does a look back over the year show us? The antinuclear composition of the overall picture stands out despite the whole complexity and diversity of the Asian and Pacific scene, despite all the hues in the distribution of light and dark tones.

Here are some of its features: The South Pacific forum elaborated on the Rarotonga treaty. Indonesia is actively promoting the concept of a nuclear-free zone in Southeast Asia. Australia and New Zealand are firmly opposed to French nuclear tests in the South Pacific and enjoy the support of the world's broad public. There are growing demands to rid the Korean peninsula of nuclear weapons. Municipalities and cities in many countries proclaim themselves nuclear-free regions. There are cases of entire states taking this stance. The Philippines and several others have included antinuclear provisions in their basic laws. The PRC is increasingly actively speaking out on disarmament problems.

In connection with the USSR-U.S. talks, Asian countries have expressed interest in the complete elimination of medium-range missiles not only in Europe but also in Asia. They are examining this question in the context of their own national security.

The Soviet leadership has adopted an entirely serious and responsible attitude toward these wishes.

And I can now announce: The Soviet Union, going halfway to meet the Asian countries and taking into account their concern, is prepared to destroy all its medium-range missiles also in the Asian part of the country; that is, it is prepared to remove the issue of retaining the 100 warheads on medium-range missiles that are being discussed at the Geneva talks with the Americans, provided, of course, the United States does the same thing. Operational and tactical missiles will also be eliminated.

In other words, we will proceed from the concept of "global double zero."

In this case, we do not link this initiative with the U.S. nuclear presence in Korea, the Philippines, and the island of Diego Garcia. But we would like to hope that there will be no buildup of this presence. . . .

Question: What measures to lessen tension in Asia and the Pacific do you consider the most pressing and practicable?

Answer: First and foremost, it is necessary again and again to talk about nuclear weapons.

Some 18 months ago we put forward a program for the phased, total elimination of nuclear weapons everywhere by the year 2000. On this basis a conceptual breakthrough was possible at the Soviet-American summit meeting in Reykjavik. For the first time people saw a prospect of a nuclear-free world.

They tried to block it. We did not agree to that. We put forward additional initiatives, which made it possible to transfer the preparation of an agreement on medium-range missiles and operational and tactical missiles onto a practical footing.

I have just announced our new step relating directly to the Asian and Pacific region.

I will also mention certain other possible measures.

First. The Soviet Union is prepared to pledge not to build up the number of nuclear-capable aircraft in the Asian part of the country provided the United States does not additionally site nuclear means there which are capable of reaching USSR territory.

Second. Once again, I remind you of our readiness to lessen the activity of the USSR and U.S. navies in the Pacific Ocean. I spoke of this in Vladivostok. But the United States has given no reply. Yet it is obvious that the border of confrontation runs through the area where the fleets are in proximity. Hence the danger of conflicts.

It would be possible to agree to limit the areas where ships carrying nuclear weapons could navigate so that they could not approach the coast of any side within the operational range of their on-board nuclear systems.

It would be possible to agree to limit antisubmarine rivalry and to ban antisubmarine activity, including aircraft activity, within specified zones.

Confidence-building would be promoted by limiting the scale of naval exercises and maneuvers in the Pacific and Indian Oceans and the adjacent seas to not more than one or two major naval (including naval aviation) exercises or maneuvers a year, notification of them in good time, and the mutual renunciation of naval exercises and maneuvers in international straits and adjacent regions and of the use of combat weapons in the zones of traditional sea routes during exercises.

It would be possible to try out this "model" first in the Northern Pacific, where there are not many "dramatis personae," and then to extend this practice to the southern part of the Pacific Sea area and other countries in the region.

Third. The UN declaration on transforming the Indian Ocean into a peace zone was adopted more than 15 years ago. Preparations have been under way for some years now for convening an international conference on the Indian Ocean, under UN auspices. It is now scheduled for 1988. But there is still no certainty that it will take place because experience shows that as soon as there is any progress here, Washington breaks off the talks.

It is time to create international guarantees for the security of shipping in the Indian Ocean and in the seas, straits, and gulfs which it contains. There is also the question of the security of air communications. This too can be resolved, given the political will. The question of collective measures against terrorism on sea and air routes in the Indian Ocean remains pressing. . . .

Question: In the Vladivostok speech you voiced the idea of convening—albeit as a distant goal—a Pacific conference with the participation of all countries oriented toward the ocean, on the model of the Helsinki conference on security and cooperation in Europe. The reaction to this idea in Asia and in the Pacific countries was mixed. What is your approach to this question now?

Answer: I spoke of this in Vladivostok as a kind of working hypothesis, or, more accurately, an invitation to discussion. I only referred to Helsinki because as yet the world community has no other experience of this kind. This does not mean, of course, that the European experience can automatically be transplanted to Asian and Pacific soil.

Nowadays, however, any international experiment has features for all of humanity and the globe. And that is only natural because we are living in an interdependent and in many respects integrated world.

Take the Delhi Declaration on the principles of a world free of nuclear weapons and violence. This is a completely new example of a political-philosophical approach to the fundamental problems of interstate contacts. This document goes far beyond bilateral and regional frameworks—it expresses the aspirations of all mankind even though it is the result of the development of relations between two countries.

Relations between India and the USSR may be termed exemplary in many senses—in being filled with diverse political, economic, scientific and technical, and cultural content, in profound mutual respect and sympathy between the two countries' peoples, and in their tone, which reflects reciprocal trust combined with a profound mutual need for friendship.

Why have relations of such a high caliber been able to develop between India and the Soviet Union, states with different sociopolitical systems? Because both sides—not in words but in deeds—base their policy on the sovereignty, equality of rights, noninterference in internal affairs, cooperation, and the recognition of each people's freedom to choose its own political system and own forms of social development.

For that very reason we also say with a sense of pride that the Soviet Union and India are creating such a valuable model of interstate relations that they may be an attractive example for others.

The Indian festival now being held in the USSR, which is unique in its scale and is imbued with the ideals of peace and goodness, just like the upcoming Soviet festival in India, embodies the present and the future of just such relations between our states and peoples.

Question: I should now like to touch on the theme of regional conflicts. Could you dwell on this?

Answer: This is a big and complex question. Each regional conflict has its own roots, its own "case history," so to speak, and its own specific cure.

I shall try to illustrate that by reference to the example of Afghanistan, where the policy of national reconciliation, which the Afghan leadership is consistently pursuing, is gradually changing the situation in the country. Entire rebel groups are ceasing their combat actions, and refugees are returning to their abandoned homes. The number of those who have returned would be much greater had the Pakistani and Iranian authorities not placed obstacles in the refugees' way. The idea of creating a coalition government has been debated, an idea which presupposes the division of power among all the forces who support or who are prepared to support internal peace and the ending of bloodshed. A law has been passed permitting the activity of political parties. The country's draft new constitution is being submitted for nationwide discussion.

All this creates the conditions for the establishment of peace in Afghanistan. Failing to see that is tantamount to not wanting a settlement of the Afghan question.

National reconciliation in Afghanistan is of course a matter solely for the Afghans themselves, including those Afghans who find themselves beyond the country's borders. The need there is for dialogue, talks, and greater trust between the opposing sides.

In principle the question of the withdrawal of the Soviet troops from Afghanistan has already been decided. We favor a speeding up of the withdrawal. However, the interference in Afghanistan's internal affairs must be ended and the nonresumption of this interference guaranteed.

Then there is the Cambodian problem. Some encouraging signs of the possibility of a settlement seem to have appeared. The understanding that this question can only be solved by political means has become established. A specific deadline has been fixed for the withdrawal of the Vietnamese troops, and we are confident that it will be observed. But the most important thing, in our view, is that the idea of national consensus is slowly but surely gaining ground. Here, too, dialogue must prevail over confrontation. Here, too, a coalition of national forces is possible.

In this context I believe that the Asian countries can also make their own not inconsiderable contribution to the incipient process. We are aware of the initiatives put forward by Indonesia and some other countries, and we welcome them.

We express solidarity with the DPRK's policy, which is aimed at the peaceful unification of the country and the removal of military tension. We also understand the desire of South Korea's population to rid themselves of foreign troops and military bases together with their nuclear weapons. . . .

Question: Everyone is well aware of the great significance of Soviet-Chinese relations for international peace and security, particularly in Asia. How have they been developing recently?

Answer: Our relations with the PRC are characterized by a gradual broadening of contacts. A noticeable improvement has appeared in the development of trade-economic, scientific-technical, and cultural ties, and great reserves have been found in all these spheres. Political dialogue is also in progress. Consultations are under way and talks on border questions have resumed.

The two nuclear powers in Asia—the USSR and the PRC—have assumed a commitment not to be first to use nuclear weapons. The Asian and Pacific countries cannot be indifferent to the question of whether or not the other nuclear powers eventually adopt a similar commitment.

Question: How do you assess the development of the Soviet Union's relations with Japan?

Answer: Their state is not very certain at the moment. In recent years efforts have been made to impart momentum to them and create a normal climate in these relations. I believe that both sides have incentives for doing this—and not only economic incentives. The Soviet Union and Japan could establish a serious, solid partnership which, I am sure, would be a significant factor of stability in the Asian-Pacific region as a whole.

Not so long ago there seemed to be a ray of hope, and discussion even began about my visiting Japan. I was inwardly prepared to visit that remarkable country, which plays a tremendous part in the world economy and is playing an increasingly notable part in world politics. But there were forces in Japan which managed to drive dark clouds up over the horizon again.

Question: How do you view the USSR's role in the development of regional economic cooperation?

Answer: Normal economic contacts can and must be developed on the basis of healthy, civilized relations of all kinds, be they general political, diplomatic, or simply human. Unfortunately, we have encountered more than once a situation where our wish to establish good relations or even simply diplomatic and trade relations with a particular country has been placed in the category of perfidious political intrigues. Sometimes the big guns of political pressure are used in an effort to intimidate the governments and public of small states which are still finding their footings.

Can you imagine the Soviet Union's protesting against the U.S. or British establishment of normal relations with Pacific Island or other states?

It is absurd: we have never done so, and we would not do so. We do not develop our relations with anyone at the expense of third countries' interests. The best and only sound basis for international relations is equality, mutual respect, noninterference in internal affairs, and mutual advantage. The Soviet National Committee for Asian-Pacific Economic Cooperation which we are setting up at the moment will serve this very purpose.

I also want to say the following. In accordance with the concept of the country's accelerated socioeconomic development—especially since the CPSU Central Committee June Plenum—we have been paying heightened attention to the territories on the other side of the Urals whose economic potential is several times greater than that of the European part of the USSR.

Joint firms and enterprises, set up in cooperation with business circles in countries of the Asian-Pacific region could participate in the development of resources in these areas.

For us the idea of universal security incorporates international economic security. An analysis of the available potential convinces us that the best way to achieve this is to implement the principle of "disarmament for development."

For the moment it might be possible to implement a program of immediate action to ease the developing world's debt burden. It might include the resumption of the net inflow of financial resources into the developing countries and, as far as possible, the removal of private bank abuses from the area of international credit. We believe the way to do this is to expand interstate aid to these countries on preferential terms.

Question: Finally, I would like to know your opinion of Soviet-Indonesian relations and of the part Indonesia is playing in modern world politics. . . .

Answer: Indonesia—a dynamically developing state, a member of the nonaligned movement and ASEAN, an active participant in the solution of many world and regional problems—will, we are sure, play an ever-growing role. We believe that Indonesia, as one of the world's biggest states and now the fifth-most-populous power, will have many important contributions to make to international politics. . . .

Appendix E
Gorbachev Issues Seven
New Peace Proposals

Krasnoyarsk. September 16, 1988. TASS.

"As a result of reflections and an additional analysis and striving to further the cause of all-Asian security, the Soviet leadership is coming forward with some new proposals," Mikhail Gorbachev, general secretary of the CPSU Central Committee, stated today.

Speaking at a meeting with party and local-government leaders, economic executives, and representatives of the public of Krasnoyarsk Territory, he read out seven new Soviet peace proposals which are aimed at strengthening security in the Asia-Pacific region.

First. Aware of the Asian and Pacific countries' concern, the Soviet Union will not increase the amount of any nuclear weapons in the region—it has already been practising this for some time—and is calling upon the United States and other nuclear powers not to deploy them additionally in the region.

Second. The Soviet Union is inviting the main naval powers of the region to hold consultations on non-increase in naval forces in the region.

Third. The USSR is suggesting that the question of lowering military confrontation in the areas where the coasts of the USSR, the PRC, Japan, the DPRK, and South Korea converge be discussed on a multilateral basis with a view to freezing and commensurately lowering the levels of naval and air forces and limiting their activity.

Fourth. If the United States agree[s] to the elimination of military bases in the Philippines, the Soviet Union will be ready, by agreement with the government of the Socialist Republic of Vietnam, to give up the fleet's material and technical supply station in Cam Ranh Bay.

Fifth. In the interests of the safety of sea lanes and air communications of the region, the USSR suggests that measures be jointly elaborated to prevent incidents in the open sea and air space above it. The experience of the already existing bilateral Soviet-American and Soviet-British accords as well as the USA-USSR-Japan trilateral accord could be used during the elaboration of these measures.

Sixth. The Soviet Union proposes that an international conference on making the Indian Ocean a zone of peace be held not later than 1990. Preparatory work for it is known to have been completed, in the main, at the United Nations organization.

Seventh. The USSR suggests discussing at any level and in any composition the question of creating a negotiating mechanism to consider Soviet and any other proposals pertaining to the security of the Asia-Pacific region. The discussion could be started between the USSR, the PRC, and the United States as permanent members of the United Nations Security Council.

Appendix F
Gorbachev Message to Aquino

Moscow. December 14, 1987. *Pravda*.
To Her Excellency Mrs Corazon C. Aquino, chairman of the third ASEAN summit meeting and president of the Republic of the Philippines.

Esteemed Madame Chairman!

In connection with the third meeting of the state and government heads of the ASEAN countries, allow me to greet you and all its participants.

The present meeting of the ASEAN countries' leaders is taking place at a crucial time when hopeful signs have emerged of an improvement in the international situation, when mankind has been presented with real opportunities for embarking on the elimination of nuclear weapons and removal of the threat of nuclear catastrophe. The signing of the Soviet-American Treaty on the Elimination of Medium- and Shorter-Range Missiles is the first big step in the matter of real disarmament. It paves the way for important new accords on strengthening peace and security.

In the minds and hearts of millions of people in the world, anxiety is still strong in connection with the continuing arms race, the tension in many parts of the world, and the exacerbation of the developing countries' financial and economic difficulties, which are hampering their struggle to strengthen political and economic independence. In our view, further persistent efforts are needed to ensure that the positive advances in the current world situation develop into a stable trend leading to a nuclear-free, nonviolent, just world.

Madame Chairman!

The Soviet Union is following ASEAN's activity with interest and sympathy, and pays tribute to the positive results achieved by the member countries in the course of national construction and the organization of cooperation within the framework of the association. Having announced 20 years ago a course of economic, social and cultural progress, the association's countries have overcome considerable difficulties and made marked progress in the implementing [of] the set targets.

We value the ASEAN states' efforts to preserve peace, ease international tension, and bring about disarmament. We note the attention paid in the ASEAN countries to the Soviet Union's proposals on the problems of the Asian-Pacific region put forward in Vladivostok and in the MERDEKA interview. We appreciate the support for the Soviet initiatives in the United Nations and at other international forums where our countries are cooperating very fruitfully.

For our part, we recognize the considerable positive potential of such constructive proposals as the concept of transforming Southeast Asia into a zone of peace, freedom, and neutrality. The Soviet side has on more than one occasion expressed its positive attitude toward the desire of the ASEAN countries and other states in the region to create a nuclear-free zone in Southeast Asia. The practical implementation of these questions would be a substantial contribution to the normalization of the situation in that part of Asia.

Without doubt, the establishment of a lasting and stable peace in Southeast Asia would be aided in many respects by the disentangling politically of the conflict situation concerning Cambodia. We are deeply convinced that the situation in that region requires radical improvement and we are doing all we can to bring this about. We welcome any constructive efforts and initiatives leading to a solution of this problem of importance to the Asian-Pacific region. For its part, the Soviet Union is prepared to continue making its own contribution in promoting the implementation of practical steps to eliminate regional tension.

It is our firm belief that the organization of extensive equal and mutually advantageous cooperation among all Asian states is a reliable guarantee of the elimination of the threat of war and the improvement of the political climate in Asia and the Pacific basin. It is the correct way to establish trust and mutual understanding among the peoples.

I want to reemphasize that the Soviet Union is open to various, including collective, forms of mutual relations with the ASEAN countries and is willing to maintain relations with the association as such.

Respectfully yours,
M. Gorbachev

Appendix G
Mikhail Gorbachev's Article
for *Pravda* and *Izvestia*

September 17, 1987

The last quarter of the 20th century has been marked by changes in the material aspect of being—changes revolutionary in their content and significance. For the first time in its history, mankind became capable of resolving many problems that had been hindering its progress over the centuries. From the standpoint of the existing and newly created resources and technologies, there are no impediments to feeding the population of many billions of people, from giving them education, providing them with housing and keeping them healthy. Given the obvious differences and potential of peoples and countries, there is now the prospect for ensuring living conditions for the inhabitants of the earth.

At the same time dangers have emerged which put into question the very existence of the human race. This is why new rules of coexistence on our unique planet are badly needed, and they should conform to the new requirements and the changed conditions.

Alas, many influential forces continue adhering to outdated concepts concerning ways to ensure national security. As a result, the world is in an absurd situation whereby persistent efforts are being made to convince it that the road to an abyss is the most correct one

It would be difficult to appraise in any other way the point of view that nuclear weapons make it possible to avert a world war. It is not simple to refute it precisely because it is totally unfounded, for one has to dispute something which is being passed off as an axiom—since no world war has broken out after the emergence of nuclear weapons, obviously it is these weapons which have averted it. It seems that it is more correct to say that a world war has been averted despite the existence of nuclear weapons.

Some time back the sides had several scores of atomic bombs apiece. Then each came to possess hundreds of nuclear missiles, and finally, the arsenals grew to include several thousand nuclear warheads. Not so long ago Soviet

132

and American scientists specifically studied the issue of the relationship between the strategic stability and the size of the nuclear arsenals. They arrived at the unanimous conclusion that 95 percent of all nuclear arms of the U.S. and the USSR can be eliminated without stability being disrupted. This is a killing argument against the "nuclear deterrence" strategy that gives birth to a mad logic. We believe that the five percent should not be retained either, and then the stability will be qualitatively different.

Not laying claims to instructing anyone, and having come to realize that mere statements about the dangerous situation in the world are unproductive, we began seeking an answer to the question of whether it was possible to have a model for ensuring national security which would not be fraught with the threat of a worldwide catastrophe.

Such an approach was in the mainstream of the concepts that had taken shape during the process of evolving the new political thinking, which is permeated with a realistic view of what is happening around us, and a realistic view of ourselves, a view characterized by an unbiased attitude toward others and an awareness of our own responsibility and security.

The new thinking is the bridging of the gap between the word and the deed. And we embarked on practical deeds. Being confident that nuclear weapons are the greatest evil and the most horrible threat, we announced a unilateral moratorium on nuclear tests, which we observed, let me put it straight, longer than we could have done, then came the January 15, 1986, statement putting forth a concrete program for stage-by-stage elimination of nuclear weapons. At the meeting with President Reagan in Reykjavik, we came close to the realization of the desirability and possibility of complete nuclear disarmament. And then we took steps which made it easier to approach an agreement on the elimination of two classes of nuclear arms—medium, and shorter-range missiles. We believe that it is possible and realistic.

While thinking of advancing toward a nuclear weapon-free world, it is essential to see to it even now that security be ensured in the process of disarmament, at each of its stages, and to think not only about that, but also to agree on mechanisms for maintaining peace at drastically reduced levels of non-nuclear armaments.

All these questions were included in proposals set forth jointly by the USSR and other socialist countries at the United Nations—the proposals for the establishment of a comprehensive system of international peace and security.

What should this be like, as we see it?

The security plan proposed by us provides, above all, for continuity and concord with the existing institutions for the maintenance of peace. The system could function on the basis of the UN Charter and within the framework of the United Nations. In our view, its ability to function will be ensured by the strict observance of the Charter's demands, additional unilateral obligations of states, as well as confidence measures and international cooperation in all spheres—political-military, economic, ecological, humanitarian and others.

I do not venture to predict how the comprehensive security system would appear in its final form. It is only clear that it can become a reality only if all means of mass annihilation are destroyed. We propose that all this be studied by an independent commission of experts and specialists which would submit its conclusions to the United Nations organization.

Personally, I have no doubt about the capability of sovereign states to assume obligations in the field of international security now. Many states are already doing this. As is known, the Soviet Union and the People's Republic of China have stated that they will not be the first to use nuclear arms. The Soviet-American agreements on nuclear armaments are another example. They contain a conscious choice of restraint and self-limitation in the most sensitive sphere of relations between the USSR and the United States. Or take the Nuclear Nonproliferation Treaty. What is it? It is a unique example of a high sense of responsibility of states.

In the present-day reality there already exist bricks from which one can start building the future system of security.

The sphere of the reasonable, responsible and rational organization of international affairs is expanding before our very eyes, though admittedly timidly. Previously unknown standards of openness, of the scope and depth of mutual monitoring and verification of compliance with adopted obligations, are being established. An American inspection team has visited an area where Soviet troops exercises are held, a group of United States congressmen has inspected the Krasnoyarsk radar station, American scientists have installed and adjusted their instruments in the area of the Soviet nuclear testing range. Soviet and American observers are now present at each other's military exercises. Annual plans of military activity are being published in accordance with agreements within the framework of the Helsinki process.

I do not know a weightier and more impressive argument in support of the fact that the situation is changing than the stated readiness of a nuclear power to voluntarily renounce nuclear weapons. References to a striving to replace them with conventional armaments, in which there supposedly exists an imbalance between NATO and the Warsaw Treaty organization in the latter's favor, are unjustified. If an imbalance or disproportions exist, let us remove them. We do not tire of repeating this, and we have proposed concrete ways of solving this problem.

In all these issues the Soviet Union is a pioneer and shows that its words are matched by its deeds.

On the question of the comparability of defense spending, here we will have to put in more work. I think that given the proper effort, within the next two or three years we will be able to compare the figures that are of interest to us and our partners and would symmetrically reflect the expenditures of the sides.

The Soviet-American talks on nuclear and space arms, the convention on the prohibition of chemical weapons, which is close to being concluded, will intensify, I am sure, the advance to detente and disarmament.

An accord on defense strategy and military sufficiency could impart a powerful impulse in this direction. These notions presuppose such a structure of the armed forces of a state that they would be sufficient to repulse a possible aggression but would not be sufficient for the conduct of offensive actions. The first step toward this could be a controlled withdrawal of nuclear and other offensive weapons from the borders with a subsequent creation along borders of strips of rarefied armaments and demilitarized zones between potential, let us put it this way, adversaries, while in principle we should work for the dissolution of military blocs and the liquidation of bases on foreign territories and the return home of all troops stationed abroad.

The question of a possible mechanism to prevent the outbreak of a nuclear conflict is more complex. Here I approach the most sensitive point of the idea of comprehensive security system. Much will have to be additionally thought out, rethought and worked out. In any case, the international community should work out agreed-upon measures in the event of a violation of the comprehensive security system agreement on the non-use and elimination of nuclear arms or an attempt to violate this agreement. As to potential nuclear piracy, it appears possible and necessary to consider this in advance and prepare collective measures to prevent it.

If the system is sufficiently effective, then it will provide even more effective guarantees of averting and curbing a non-nuclear aggression.

The system proposed by us precisely presupposes definite measures which would enable the United Nations organization, the main universal security body, to ensure its maintenance at a level of reliability.

II

The division of the world's countries into those possessing nuclear weapons and those not possessing them has also split the very concept of security. But for human life security is indivisible. In this sense it is not only a political, military and legal, but also a moral, category. And contentions that there has been no war for already half a century do not withstand any test on the touchstone of ethics. How can one say there is no war? There are dozens of regional wars flaring up in the world.

It is immoral to treat this as secondary. The matter, however, is not only in the impermissible nuclear elitism. The elimination of nuclear weapons would also be a major step toward a genuine democratization of relations between states, their equality and equal responsibility.

Unconditional observance of the United Nations Charter and the right of peoples sovereignly to choose the roads and forms of their development, revolutionary or evolutionary, is an imperative condition of universal security. This applies also to the right to social status quo. This, too, is exclusively an internal matter. Any attempts, direct or indirect, to influence the development of "not one of our own" countries, to interfere in this development, should be ruled out. Just as impermissible are attempts to destabilize existing governments from outside.

At the same time the world community cannot stay away from conflicts between states. Here it could be possible to begin by fulfilling the proposal made by the United Nations Secretary-General to set up under the United Nations organization a multilateral center for lessening the danger of war. Clearly it would be feasible to consider the expediency of setting up a direct communication line between the United Nations headquarters and the capitals of the countries that are permanent members of the Security Council and the location of the chairman of the nonaligned movement.

It appears to us that with the aim of strengthening trust and mutual understanding it could be possible to set up under the aegis of the United Nations a mechanism for extensive international verification of compliance with agreements to lessen international tension, limit armaments and to monitor the military situation in conflict areas. The mechanism would function using various forms and methods of monitoring to collect information, and would promptly submit it to the United Nations. This would make it possible to have an objective picture of the events taking place, to detect preparations for hostilities in time, impede a sneak attack, take measures to avert an armed conflict and prevent it from expanding and becoming worse.

We are arriving at the conclusion that wider use should be made of the institution of United Nations military observers and United Nations peace-keeping forces in disengaging the troops of warring sides and observing ceasefire and armistice agreements.

And, of course at all stages of a conflict extensive use should be made of all means of a peaceful settlement of disputes and differences between states, and one should offer one's good offices, one's mediation with the aim of achieving an armistice. The ideas and initiatives concerning nongovernmental commissions and groups which would analyze the causes, circumstances and methods of resolving various concrete conflict situations appear to be fruitful.

The Security Council's permanent members could become guarantors of regional security. On their part, they could assume the obligation not to use force or the threat of force, to renounce demonstrative military presence. This is so because such a practice is one of the factors fanning regional conflicts.

A drastic intensification and expansion of the cooperation of states in uprooting international terrorism is extremely important. It would be expedient to concentrate this cooperation within the framework of the United Nations organization. In our opinion, it would be useful to create under its aegis a tribunal to investigate acts of international terrorism.

More coordination in the struggle against apartheid as a destabilizing factor of international magnitude would also be justified.

As we see it, all the above-stated measures could be organically built into a comprehensive system of peace and security.

III

The events and tendencies of the past decades have expanded this concept, imparting new features and specificities to it. One of them is the problem of economic security. A world in which a whole continent can find itself on the brink of death from starvation and in which huge masses of people are suffering from almost permanent malnutrition is not a safe world. Neither is a world safe in which a multitude of countries and peoples are strangling in a noose of debt.

The economic interests of individual countries or their groups are indeed so different and contradictory that consensus with regard to the concept of the new world economic order seems to be hard to achieve. We do hope, however, that the instinct of self-preservation should snap into action here as well. It is sure to manifest itself if it becomes possible to look into the chain of priorities and see that there are circumstances, menacing in their inevitability, and that it is high time that the inert political mentality inherited from the past views of the outside world be abandoned. This world has ceased to be a sphere which the big and strong divide into domains and zones of vital interests.

The imperatives of the times compel us to institutionalize many common sense notions. It is not philanthropy which prompted our proposal to agree on the reduction of interest payments under bank credits and the elaboration of extra benefits for the least developed nations. This holds a benefit for all, namely a secure future. If the debt burden of the developing world is alleviated, the chances for such a future will grow. It is also possible to limit debt payments by each developing country to the share of its annual export earnings without detriment to development, to accept export commodities in payment for the debt, remove protectionist barriers on the borders of creditor-nations and stop adding extra interest when deferring payments under debts.

There may be different attitudes toward these proposals. There is no doubt, however, that the majority of international community members realize the need for immediate actions to alleviate the developing world's debt burden. If that is so, it is possible to start working out the program through concerted efforts.

These words "through concerted efforts" are very important for today's world. The relationship between disarmament and development, confirmed at the recent international conference in New York, can be implemented if none of the strong and rich keep themselves aloof. I already expressed the view that Security Council member states, represented by their top officials, could jointly discuss this problem and work out a coordinated approach. I confirm this proposal.

Ecological security. It is not secure in the direct meaning of the word when currents of poison flow along river channels, when poisonous rains pour down from the sky, when the atmosphere polluted with industrial and transport waste chokes cities and whole regions, when the development of atomic engineering is used to justify taking unacceptable risks.

Many have suddenly begun to perceive all that not as something abstract, but as quite a real part of their own experience. The confidence that "this won't affect us," characteristic of the past outlook, has disappeared. They say that one thorn of experience is worth more than a whole forest of instructions. For us, Chernobyl became such a thorn.

The relationship between man and the environment has become menacing.

Problems of ecological security affect everyone—the rich and the poor. What is required is the global strategy of environmental protection and the rational use of resources. We suggest starting its elaboration within the framework of the UN special program.

States are already exchanging appropriate information and are notifying international organizations of developments. We believe that this procedure should be formalized by introducing the principle of governments giving annual reports about their conservationist activity and about ecological accidents, both those that occurred and those that were prevented on the territory of their countries.

Realizing the need for opening a common front of economic and ecological security and starting its formation mean defusing a delayed-action bomb planted deep inside humanity's existence by history, by the people themselves. . . .

V

The suggested system of comprehensive security will be effective to the extent to which the United Nations, its Security Council, and other international institutes and mechanisms effectively function. It will be required to enhance resolutely the authority and role of the UN, the International Atomic Energy Agency. The need for establishing a world space organization is clearly felt. In the future it could work in close contact with the UN as an autonomous part of its system. UN specialized agencies should also become regulators of international processes. The Geneva Disarmament Conference should become a forum that would internationalize the efforts on transition to a nuclear-free, nonviolent world.

One should not forget the capacities of the International Court [of Justice] either. The General Assembly and the Security Council could approach it more often for consultative conclusions on international disputes. Its mandatory jurisdiction should be recognized by all on mutually agreed-upon conditions. The permanent members of the Security Council, taking into account their special responsibility, should make the first steps in that direction.

We are convinced that a comprehensive system of security is, at the same time, a system of universal law and order ensuring the primacy of international law in politics.

The UN Charter gives extensive powers to the Security Council. Joint efforts are required to ensure that it can use them effectively. For this purpose, it would be sensible to hold meetings of the Security Council at the foreign ministers' level when opening a regular session of the General Assembly to review the international situation and jointly look for effective ways to improve it.

It would be useful to hold meetings of the Security Council not only at the headquarters of the UN in New York, but also in regions of friction and tension and alternate them among the capitals of the permanent member states.

Special missions of the Council to regions of actual and potential conflicts would also help consolidate its authority and enhance the effectiveness of the decisions adopted.

In our view, it is important to hold special sessions of the General Assembly on the more urgent political problems and individual disarmament issues more often if its efficiency is to be improved.

We emphatically stress the need for making the status of important political documents passed by consensus at the United Nations more binding morally and politically. Let me recall that they include, among others, the final document of the First Special Session of the United Nations General Assembly Devoted to Disarmament, the Charter of Economic Rights and Obligations of States, and others.

In our opinion, we should have set up long ago a world consultative council under UN auspices uniting the world's top intellectuals. Prominent scientists, political and public figures, representatives of international public organizations, cultural workers, people in literature and the arts, including laureates of the Nobel Prize and other international prizes of worldwide significance, and eminent representatives of the churches could seriously enrich the spiritual and ethical potential of contemporary world politics.

To ensure that the United Nations and its specialized agencies operate at full capacity, one should come to realize that it is impermissible to use financial levers for bringing pressure to bear on it. The Soviet Union will continue to cooperate actively in overcoming budget difficulties arising at the United Nations. . . .

Notes

Introduction

1. John J. Stephan, "Asia in the Soviet Conception," in *Soviet Policy in East Asia,* ed. Donald Zagoria (New Haven: Yale University Press, 1982).

2. Mikhail Gorbachev, *Perestroika* (New York: Harper and Row, 1987), p. 180.

Chapter 1

1. CINCPAC briefing for author, Honolulu, March 1988.

2. Tokyo, Ministry of Foreign Affairs, January 1988.

3. Bruce Stokes, "New Rivals in Asia," *National Journal,* May 9, 1988, pp. 1116-18.

4. See Robert A. Manning, "Reagan's Chance Hit," *Foreign Policy,* Spring 1984.

5. See Jonathan Pollack, "The Lessons of Coalition Politics" (Santa Monica, Calif., Rand Corporation, 1984). This provides a detailed history of security relations between the United States and the People's Republic of China examined from the view of Beijing's calculations, and explains U.S. miscalculations.

6. See Richard Nations, "A Tilt Toward Tokyo," *Far Eastern Economic Review,* April 23, 1983. Also, James Auer, "Japan's Defense Policy," *Current History,* April 1988.

7. See Harry Gelman, "The Soviet Far East Build-Up and Soviet Risk-Taking Against China" (Santa Monica, Calif., Rand Corporation, August 1982). This is an incisive analysis of the Sino-Soviet conflict.

8. See Richard H. Solomon and Masatuka Kosaka, eds., *The Soviet Far East Military Build-up* (Dover, Mass.: Auburn House, 1986). This is the best detailed discussion of the subject, esp. chaps. 2 and 3.

9. See "Defense of Japan," *JDA,* 1984. Also Solomon and Kosaka, *Soviet Far East Military Build-up,* chap. 3.

10. CINCPAC briefing, Honolulu, March 1988.

11. William T. Tow, "Nuclear Security Problems in the Far East," *Asia-Pacific Community,* Winter 1983.

12. "East Asia, the West, and International Security" (London: International Institute for Strategic Studies, Adelphi Paper no. 216, spring 1987.

13. U.S. Department of State, East Asia Bureau, 1988.

Chapter 2

1. Mikhail Gorbachev, *Perestroika* (New York: Harper and Row, 1987), pp. 18-19.

2. See Francis Fukuyama, "Moscow Post-Brezhnev Reassessment of the Third World" (Santa Monica, Calif., Rand Corporation, 1986). This is the best discussion of the evolution of Soviet thinking.

3. A. Bovin, "Restructuring and Foreign Policy," *Izvestia*, June 16, 1988.

4. Fukuyama, "Moscow Post-Brezhnev Reassessment."

5. Leonid Brezhnev, Report of the CPSU Central Committee, in *FBIS-Soviet*, February 24, 1981.

6. *Kommunist*, no. 9, June 1983.

7. Charles Wolf et al., "The Costs of Soviet Empire" (Santa Monica, Calif., Rand Corporation, 1983).

8. *New York Times*, December 4, 1987.

9. Gorbachev, *Perestroika*, pp. 135-50.

10. *Pravda*, August 6, 1988, p. 2.

11. See *Pravda*, August 11, 1988, and August 13, 1988. Two speeches answering Ligachev.

12. *Economist*, March 26, 1988.

13. *Le Monde*, September 7, 1988.

14. See Francis Fukuyama, "Soviet Political Perspectives on Power-Projection" (Santa Monica, Calif., Rand Corporation, March 1987).

15. *Pravda*, February 2, 1982.

16. *Kommunist*, no. 16, November 1986.

17. *Pravda*, July 14, 1987.

18. Michael MacGuire, "Military Objectives in Soviet Foreign Policy" (Washington, D.C.: Brookings Institution, 1987). Also in *World Policy Journal*, Spring 1987.

19. *Pravda*, May 30, 1987.

20. See R. Jeffrey Smith, *Washington Post*, August 1, 1988, p. 1. Also Raymond Garthoff, "New Thinking in Soviet Military Doctrine," *The Washington Quarterly*, Summer 1988, for an exhaustive discussion of the various strands of Soviet thinking on defense.

21. *Pravda*, September 25, 1988.

Chapter 3

1. *Pravda*, July 29, 1986.

2. Ibid.

3. *Pravda*, April 24, 1986.

4. *Pravda*, July 29, 1986.

5. Ibid.

6. *Asahi Evening News,* May 29, 1987.

7. *Economist,* May 25, 1985, pp. 88-91.

8. See T. Shabad in U.S. Congress, Joint Economic Committee, *Gorbachev's Economic Plans* (Washington, D.C.: Government Printing Office, 1987), vol. 2.

9. *Pravda,* April 24, 1986.

10. See Victor L. Mote, "Regional Planning: The BAM and the Pyramids of Power," in *Gorbachev's Economic Plans,* vol. 2, pp. 368-82.

11. Ibid.

12. Ibid.

13. See Richard Nations, "Moscow's New Tack," *Far Eastern Economic Review,* August 14, 1986. Also, author's interview with Soviet official.

14. *Security in the Asia-Pacific Region,* Novosti Press Agency, Moscow, 1988, pp. 46-48.

Chapter 4

1. *Pravda,* March 25, 1982.

2. Harry Gelman, "The Soviet Far East Build-up and Soviet Risk-Taking against China" (Santa Monica, Calif., Rand Corporation, August 1982).

3. *Beijing Review,* September 15, 1986.

4. *Christian Science Monitor,* August 11, 1986.

5. *Wall Street Journal,* September 18, 1987.

6. *Sovetskaya Rossiya,* November 13, 1987, second of two-part series.

7. *Literaturnaya Gazeta,* June 15, 1986.

8. See Chong-pin Lin, *China's Nuclear Weapons Strategy* (Boston: Lexington Books, 1988). Also Robert G. Sutter, "China's Nuclear Weapons and Arms Control Policies: Implications for the United States" (Washington, D.C., Congressional Research Service, May 16, 1988).

9. U.S. Congress, Joint Economic Committee, *Chinese Economy, Post-Mao* (Washington, D.C.: Government Printing Office, 1978).

10. Gelman, "Soviet Far East Build-up."

11. Gerald Segal, *Arms Control in Asia* (New York: St. Martins Press, 1987), p. 60.

12. Deng Xiaoping, statement in *Liaowang,* September 16, 1985.

13. See Banning Garret and Bonnie Glaser, "Chinese on SDI," *Problems of Communism,* March-April 1986.

14. See Jonathan Pollack, "The Lessons of Coalition Politics" (Santa Monica, Calif., Rand Corporation, 1984).

15. *Asahi Shimbun,* May 16, 1980.

16. *Beijing Review,* January 18-24, 1980.

17. Kyodo News Service, Tokyo, May 3, 1988.

18. Zhang Liang, *Remnin Ribao,* April 12, 1988.

19. Huan Xiang, Xinhua News Service, Beijing, April 28, 1988. Qian Qichen

echoed this in a speech to the Council on Foreign Relations in New York, May 31, 1988 (printed in *Beijing Review,* June 6, 1988).

Chapter 5

1. See Fuji Kamiya, "The Northern Territories: 130 Years of Japanese Talk with Czarist Russia and the Soviet Union," in *Soviet Policy in East Asia,* ed. Donald Zagoria (New Haven: Yale University Press, 1982), chap. 5.

2. Testimony in U.S. Congress, House Foreign Affairs Committee, hearings on "The Soviet Role in Asia," July 21, 1983.

3. See Peter Berton, "Soviet-Japanese Relations," *Asian Survey,* December 1986. Excellent detailed discussion of the Shevardnadze and Abe visits.

4. TASS, Moscow, May 30, 1986 (in *FBIS-Soviet,* June 2, 1986).

5. See Susumu Awanohara, *Far Eastern Economic Review,* November 13, 1986.

6. See Gordon B. Smith, "Recent Trends in Soviet-Japanese Trade," *Problems of Communism,* January-February 1987. Also *Far Eastern Economic Review,* June 23, 1988, p. 80.

7. Moscow Radio, February 11, 1988 (in *FBIS-Soviet,* February 22, 1988).

8. *Pravda,* May 7, 1988.

9. Kyodo News Service, Tokyo, May 7, 1988.

10. Kyodo News Service, July 8, 1988.

11. *Yomiuri Shimbun,* August 9, 1988, p. 1.

12. *Yomiuri Shimbun,* July 12, 1988, p. 2.

13. Kyodo News Service, May 18, 1988, interview with Primakov.

14. *Washington Times,* June 6, 1988. Also, author's interview with U.S. officials.

15. See Selig Harrison, testimony before U.S. Congress, House Subcommittee on East Asia and the Pacific, May 24, 1988.

16. Letter from South Korean prime minister to North Korean counterpart (in *FBIS,* June 12, 1988). More elaborate proposals and exchanges were suggested by President Roh Tae Woo in a televised address on July 6, 1988 (in *FBIS-EAS,* July 7, 1988).

17. See *Washington Post,* February 23, 1988, for analysis.

18. See Selig Harrison, "The Great Follower," *Far Eastern Economic Review,* December 3, 1987.

19. See *Business Korea,* February 1988. Also *Korea Newsreview,* February 6, 1988.

20. *Korea Herald,* February 26, 1988.

Chapter 6

1. See *Pravda,* July 29, 1986.

2. *Bangkok Post,* November 21, 1987. Also, interview with Chaovalit on Moscow Radio (in *FBIS-Soviet,* December 1, 1987).

3. *Pravda,* December 14, 1987.

4. *Economist,* December 5, 1987.

5. See Carol Fogarty and Kevin Trittle, "Moscow's Economic Aid Program in LDC's," in U.S. Congress, Joint Economic Committee, *Gorbachev's Economic Plans* (Washington, D.C.: Government Printing Office, 1987), vol. 2.

6. Author's interview with U.S. official.

7. See Richard Kessler in "Outlook," *Washington Post,* July 26, 1987.

8. *Philippines Daily Inquirer,* April 23, 1988.

9. *Manila Chronicle,* March 25, 1988.

10. *Asian Wall Street Journal,* July 1, 1987.

11. Author's interview with U.S. official.

12. See Douglas Pike, *Vietnam and the USSR* (Boulder: Westview Press, 1986). Also see Robert C. Horn, "Alliance Politics between Comrades" (Santa Monica, Calif., Rand Corporation, August 1987). For the best background and analysis of post-1975 conflict, see Nayan Chanda, *Brother Enemy* (New York: Harcourt Brace, 1986).

13. *Nhan Dan,* Hanoi, June 18, 1985.

14. Nayan Chanda, "Soulmates' Dissonance," *Far Eastern Economic Review,* June 11, 1987, and "The Prince Makes Waves," *Far Eastern Economic Review,* June 18, 1987.

15. Nayan Chanda, "A Troubled Friendship," *Far Eastern Economic Review,* June 9, 1988.

16. *New York Times,* November 27, 1987.

17. Nayan Chanda, "A Troubled Friendship."

18. *New York Times,* February 8, 1988.

19. Nayan Chanda, "A Troubled Friendship."

20. *New York Times,* February 11, 1988.

Chapter 7

1. *New York Times,* March 30, 1988.

2. Mikhail Gorbachev, speech to CPSU Central Committee, February 1988 (*Washington Post,* April 17, 1988).

3. See Don Oberdorfer, *Washington Post,* April 17, 1988. This is an excellent, detailed analysis of the evolution of the Soviet decision to pull out of Afghanistan.

4. *New York Times,* December 11, 1987.

5. *New York Times,* February 11, 1988. Also, author's interviews with U.S. officials.

6. Graham Fuller in "Outlook," *Washington Post,* March 6, 1988.

7. Harry Gelman, "Gorbachev's Dilemma," *Orbis,* Summer 1986.

8. *Literaturnaya Gazeta,* February 18, 1988.

9. Interview in *Komsomolskaya Pravda,* June 19, 1988.

10. See Elizabeth Krindl Valkenier, "New Soviet Thinking about the Third World," *World Policy Journal,* Fall 1987.

11. Fuller, "Outlook," *Washington Post,* March 6, 1988.

12. George F. Kennan, "Sources of Soviet Conduct," *Foreign Affairs,* July 1947.

13. Ibid.
14. Ibid.

Chapter 8

1. See *New York Times Magazine,* July 10, 1988, for a discussion about the campaign to sell American cigarettes in Asia.

2. See Rear Admiral Edward Baker, testimony before U.S. Congress, House Subcommittee on Asia and the Pacific, September 10, 1986.

Index

Abe, Shintaro, 55-56
ADB. *See* Asian Development Bank
Afghanistan: conflict resolution, 8, 48, 60, 81-85, 88; Soviet invasion of, 13, 22, 29, 42, 55, 61, 71, 73; troop withdrawal from, 1, 23, 36, 40, 43, 77, 82, 83-84, 85, 93
Aganbegyan, Abel, 38
Airlines: attacks on, 55, 62, 64
Akhromeyev, Sergi, 29
Aliyev, Geidar, 62
Amelko, Nikolai, 58-59
Andropov, Yuri, 23, 24
Antinuclear movement, 5, 16, 67, 68, 70-71, 72-73, 92
ANZUS, 8, 9, 13, 16
Aquino, Corazon, 69, 72, 74
Arkhipov, Ivan, 42, 43
Armitage, Richard, 73-74
Arms control, 1, 23, 29, 48, 89, 92, 93, 96, 97, 98. *See also* Disarmament; Intermediate-range Nuclear Forces Treaty; Strategic Arms Reduction Talks
Arms sales, 16, 49, 68, 70, 95, 98
ASEAN. *See* Association of Southeast Asian Nations
Asian Development Bank (ADB), 25, 69, 92, 93, 98
Association of Southeast Asian Nations (ASEAN), 8, 18, 67, 68, 71, 77, 78-79, 96, 98-99; relations with the Soviet Union, 23, 30, 34, 38, 57, 68-70, 74; relations with the United States, 9, 13; relations with Vietnam, 14, 75, 97, 98
Australia, 8, 13, 18, 68

Balance of power, 3, 5-6, 14
Border disputes, 36, 40, 42, 43, 44, 48
Borders, 2, 47, 81, 85

Bovin, Aleksandr, 22
Brezhnev, Leonid, 26, 42, 99; economic policies of, 38; foreign policies of, 2, 21, 22, 29, 33, 39, 68, 89; Tashkent speech, 41-42
Brezhnev Doctrine, 23-24, 26, 27, 40, 45, 53, 81-82, 85, 92
Brunei, 8
Brutents, Karen, 22, 27-28
Brzezinski, Zbigniew, 85
Bukharin, Nikolai, 46
Bureaucracy, 45, 55; American, 95; Soviet, 29, 38-39
Burlatskiy, Fyodor, 46
Burma, 28, 64

Cambodia, 18, 67
Cambodian conflict, 42, 48, 61, 68, 73, 74-75; resolution of, 8, 16, 40, 76-78, 81, 88, 89; troop withdrawals in, 44, 74, 77
Carlucci, Frank, 29
Carter administration, 9
Chaovalit Yongchaiyut, 68
Chebrikov, Viktor, 31
Chernenko, Konstantin, 55, 62
China, 5, 78-79; defenses, 48; economic relations with the Soviet Union, 16, 42-43, 45; economy, 6, 47, 92; foreign opinion of, 14, 69; foreign relations with the Soviet Union, 22-23, 27, 30, 36, 41-49, 60, 75-76; relations with Cambodia, 48, 77, 78; relations with Japan, 17, 49-50, 55; relations with the Korean Peninsula, 61, 62, 64, 65, 66, 96; relations with the United States, 8, 10, 13, 42, 49, 51, 73, 95-96; relations with Vietnam, 16, 74, 75, 78, 97; strategic relations with the Soviet Union, 10, 11, 35, 39, 40, 57, 67, 81; trade, 16, 42-43, 51, 96